More Praise for *Boards That Excel*

"The book provides insightful discussions of the necessary skills, attitudes, and knowledge that any board member must have. It gives well-structured coverage of best board practices. It also offers contexts for those practices by including insightful personal reflections on the role a board plays in organizational leadership from one who has thought deeply about it and actually experienced it in many important organizations."

—Paul Danos, Dean and Laurence F. Whittemore Professor of Business Administration, Tuck School of Business at Dartmouth, and Director, General Mills

"Joe White and Dave Gray were the first nonfamily board members in our company's 100-year history. We attribute much of the growth and success to the insights and principles offered up in this outstanding book. Joe does not deal with the theoretical but, rather, the real and often difficult issues that boards and directors grapple with every day."

—Dan Gordon, Chairman, Gordon Food Service

"*Boards That Excel* is an essential resource for *all* directors, new and experienced, of both for-profit companies and not-for-profit organizations. It's the perfect blend of research data and real-world best practices and experience that can drive effective governance in an ever-changing environment."

—Mary Kay Haben, Director, Hershey and Bob Evans, and Trustee, Equity Residential

"*Boards That Excel* is a great book for students, investors, and directors to understand the essence of what makes companies tick. Joe White's insightful thoughts and observations can help anyone who reads them understand the impact directors and corporate governance principles can have on the corporation."

—Rick Hill, former Chairman and CEO, Novellus Systems, and Director, Arrow Electronics, LSI, Cabot Microelectronics, Tessera, and Planar Systems

"What I've come to appreciate over the years is that at the end of the day, good governance is an art. It improves with hours of practice and experience. As with the team game of basketball, one gets better sooner by studying from the masters. Joe White is a master—he is the John Wooden and Vince Lombardi of corporate governance."

—Mannie Jackson, Chairman, Boxcar Holdings; former owner and Chairman, Harlem Globetrotters; Director, Acorn Energy, EPIC Research & Diagnostics, and Arizona Diamondbacks; and former director of companies including Ashland Oil, Jostens, Reebok, Stanley Black & Decker, Transamerica, and True North

"Joe White is a leader in the increasingly important field of corporate governance. He is sought out as an advisor to major corporations, is a thought leader among academicians, and is an active participant in the boardroom. His book should be required reading for those presently sitting in the boardroom, those expecting to participate in the future, and those seeking the best thinking in the corporate governance world."

—**Sheli Rosenberg, cofounder and former Director, Center for Executive Women, Kellogg School of Management, Northwestern University, and Director, Equity LifeStyle Properties, Nanosphere, Strategic Hotels & Resorts, and Ventas**

"Joe White's book serves as a primer for new and seasoned board members. It is filled with relevant and personal anecdotes that provide valuable insights on how to function effectively on boards. It is a must-read for anyone who has said yes to a board invitation—and it should be handed out by those doing the asking."

—**Tim Solso, Chairman, General Motors; Director, Ball; and former Chairman and CEO, Cummins**

"As stewards of owners' interests, effective boards guide corporations to be creators of value. *Boards That Excel* walks readers through many critical leadership and governance issues based on the author's wealth of real-life experiences and academic knowledge. It leads caring corporate stewards to develop a comprehensive agenda on which excellent boards and directorships are built. Readers will agree that this is a 'must keep' reference book and will turn to it regularly."

—**Bernard Yeung, Dean and Stephen Riady Distinguished Professor of Finance and Strategic Management, National University of Singapore Business School, and President, Asian Bureau of Finance and Economic Research**

"Joe White's *Boards That Excel* is an in-depth effort to reconcile the importance of governance with the ultimate mission of a board of directors. Perhaps the most relevant of many insights in the book is the recognition that performance and return on investment are ultimate measures and that superior governance contributes to those positive results."

—**Sam Zell, Chairman, Equity Group Investments, Equity Residential, Equity LifeStyle Properties, Anixter, and Covanta**

BOARDS
THAT
EXCEL

BOARDS
THAT
EXCEL

Candid Insights &
Practical Advice for Directors

B. JOSEPH WHITE

Berrett–Koehler Publishers, Inc.
San Francisco
a BK Business book

Berrett-Koehler Publishers, Inc.
235 Montgomery Street, Suite 650
San Francisco, CA 94104-2916
Tel: (415) 288-0260 Fax: (415) 362-2512   www.bkconnection.com

Ordering Information
Quantity sales. Special discounts are available on quantity purchases by corporations, associations, and others. For details, contact the "Special Sales Department" at the Berrett-Koehler address above.
Individual sales. Berrett-Koehler publications are available through most bookstores. They can also be ordered directly from Berrett-Koehler: Tel: (800) 929-2929; Fax: (802) 864-7626; www.bkconnection.com
Orders for college textbook/course adoption use. Please contact Berrett-Koehler: Tel: (800) 929-2929; Fax: (802) 864-7626.
Orders by U.S. trade bookstores and wholesalers. Please contact Ingram Publisher Services, Tel: (800) 509-4887; Fax: (800) 838-1149; E-mail: customer.service@ ingrampublisherservices.com; or visit www.ingrampublisherservices.com/Ordering for details about electronic ordering.

Berrett-Koehler and the BK logo are registered trademarks
of Berrett-Koehler Publishers, Inc.

Printed in the United States of America

Berrett-Koehler books are printed on long-lasting acid-free paper. When it is available, we choose paper that has been manufactured by environmentally responsible processes. These may include using trees grown in sustainable forests, incorporating recycled paper, minimizing chlorine in bleaching, or recycling the energy produced at the paper mill.

Library of Congress Cataloging-in-Publication Data

White, B. Joseph.
Boards that excel : candid insights and practical advice for directors
B. Joseph White. -- First edition.
    pages cm
ISBN 978-1-62656-222-6 (hardback)
1. Boards of directors. 2. Corporate governance. I. Title.
HD2745.W534 2014
658.4'22--dc23

                    2014012784

First Edition
19 18 17 16 15 14   10 9 8 7 6 5 4 3 2 1

Author photo courtesy of the College of Business, University of Illinois.
Jacket design: Kirk DouPonce, DogEared Design

To Brian and Leisa White,
Audrey and Darren Imhoff
and my grandchildren—
Bernie, Hattie, Lizzie, Caleb, and Owen.

In the hope that you will live in a world
of companies and organizations governed
by wise directors and capable boards.

With love,

B. Joseph White
Champaign, Illinois
August 2014

CONTENTS

Pay It Forward

The Purpose of This Book

We are products of our experiences. Two of mine have greatly influenced the views about governance expressed in this book. In both cases, I was there at the creation. The principals involved had high aspirations and a stewardship attitude toward governance. Results over more than two decades have been strong and positive.

My boss, Dean Gil Whitaker of the University of Michigan Business School, walked into my office in Ann Arbor with a guest. "Hi, I'm Paul Gordon," he said with a deep voice and a big smile. "We have a little family business in Grand Rapids. I'm wondering if you could help us with governance and a few other things."

Paul was a graduate of the school where I was a professor and associate dean. He was in his mid-sixties when we met. Paul had recently begun to think deeply about the long-term future of Gordon Food Service (GFS), the growing private company he headed with his brother, John. Gil thought I might be able to help Paul because I had just returned to the school after a six-year stint in the real world

1

at Cummins, Inc., the diesel engine and power systems company in Columbus, Indiana.

Paul and I hit it off immediately. He told me about his family and the food service business. I related some things I'd learned at Cummins about quality, leadership and change. Together, we visited GFS's new, automated distribution center in nearby Brighton, Michigan. A few weeks later, I went to Grand Rapids and met his brother, John, and their three sons in the business. I liked them and what I saw. The feeling seemed to be mutual.

I learned later that Paul was having a similar conversation with another person, David L. Gray. Dave also passed muster with the Gordons. So, at Paul's and John's request, Dave and I began to work together to help the Gordons create a modern board of directors and an orderly senior management succession process. Together, we became the first outside board members in their ninety-year old, family controlled company.

That was twenty-seven years ago. At the time, GFS had revenues of $400 million, two distribution centers, a few retail

Gordon Food Service (private)

1987	2014
• Revenue $400 million	• Revenue $10 billion
• Two distribution centers, several stores	• 20 distribution centers, 150 Marketplace stores
• Three-state market	• Eastern half of U.S., coast-to-coast in Canada
	• #34 private company

cash-and-carry stores, and a market area comprised mainly of Michigan and northern Ohio and Indiana. Today, revenues exceed $10 billion. The company has more than 20 distribution centers and 150 Marketplace stores that serve much of the U.S. and Canada. In 2013, GFS was the thirty-fourth largest private company in America in *Forbes* magazine's annual ranking. In December 2013, the employee profit sharing plan's assets exceeded $1 billion for the first time. It's been a remarkable business story.

Sam Zell called me on a summer day in 1993. By then I was dean of the University of Michigan Business School, Gil Whitaker's successor. I knew Sam; everybody at Michigan did. His one-page biography at the time began, "Sam Zell was born in Chicago and graduated from the University of Michigan." Sam liked to point out that the richer he got, the more interested the University became in him. So it was a surprise for *him* to be calling *me*.

I picked up the phone in my office.

"Joe," said Sam in his gravelly voice. "We're creating a new public company—a real estate investment trust. We believe this is a time of tremendous opportunity in the apartment business. We'll be doing an initial public offering soon. We're assembling a board of trustees. I'll be chairman. We'd like you to be a trustee."[1]

I knew, liked and trusted Sam. I recalled his sitting in my university office recounting how he and his late partner, Bob Lurie, got started in the real estate business in Ann Arbor when they were students. Sam and Bob worked briefly for Don Chisholm, a local real estate entrepreneur. It didn't take them long to figure out that they'd rather be owners than employees. So they began to buy apartments in Ann Arbor. Forty years later, Sam recounted to me the purchase of each property *in detail:* street address, owner, price, down payment, and terms of the mortgage!

After graduation, Sam and Bob set up shop in their hometown of Chicago. Over the years, their private firm, Equity Group Investments, became a major owner of apartment properties across the country. They invested in other businesses as well. But apartments were their first love.

By 1993, Sam was a legendary real estate investor. While his public persona was arresting (e.g., as the leader of Zell's Angels, buddies who rode fast motorcycles in exotic places), it was clear that he had an uncanny knack for finding value in real estate. One of Sam's monikers was the "grave dancer" in recognition of his penchant for scooping up unloved properties at rock bottom prices and making big profits on them. He also ran first class companies.

It didn't take me long to do my due diligence on EQR. I was impressed by the game plan and by members of senior management I met. So I accepted the invitation to join the board. Thus began my first adventure in the governance of a major *public* company, Equity Residential, Inc. (EQR).

Twenty-one years have passed and EQR has thrived. At the time of the initial public offering in 1993, the company owned 25,000 apartments and had an enterprise value of $800 million. Today, EQR owns over 100,000 apartments in premier properties on the east and west coasts, has an enterprise value in excess of $30 billion and is an S&P 500 company. Annualized total shareholder return since the IPO has been 13%. Like GFS, EQR has been a remarkable business story.

Equity Residential (public)

1993	**2014**
• IPO	• S&P 500 company
• 25,000 apartments	• 100,000 apartments
• $800 million value	• $35 billion value
	○ 13% TSR/20 years

GFS and EQR have grown and thrived over the last two decades. So have I—from a novice director of GFS and a new trustee of EQR to one of both boards' senior members and, at EQR, chair of the corporate governance committee. During those years, I completed a decade as dean, was the University of Michigan's interim president, and served five years as president of the University of Illinois. I also served on numerous nonprofit boards and reported to two as the chief executive officer of major public universities.

Professional school faculty at top universities get a lot of opportunities to do outside work related to their academic specialties. You have to be selective in saying "yes" because the university limits the amount you can do and your hard-earned reputation is always on the line. What attracted me to GFS and EQR were the high aspirations that both Paul Gordon and Sam Zell had for the companies they headed.

"We've been around almost a hundred years," said Paul. "We need governance that will enable us thrive forever."

"We're going to be a prodigious user of capital," said Sam when the board asked me to be the first chair of EQR's audit committee. "Your job is to make sure our credibility with the capital markets is rock solid."

The Gordons and the EQR board took a risk on me. As a business school dean and professor and former Cummins executive, I liked business and knew a fair amount about it. But I was green as a director. I also took a risk on GFS and EQR. Over the years, people have asked me whether they should join a particular board. I advise them to do proper due diligence on the company or organization involved then answer this all-important question: How do you feel about having your reputation in the hands of the company's chairman and CEO? In twenty-seven years with two chairmen and two CEO's at GFS and twenty-one years with Sam as chairman and three CEO's of EQR, my comfort has always been high.

I owe a debt of gratitude to the many people who helped me go from being a novice board member to an experienced and capable one. At the university commencements where I presided as dean and president, I always asked the graduating students to thank those on whose shoulders they stood: parents and family, teachers, coaches, counselors, friends. Now it's my turn to do the same. I thank the directors and executives of Cummins, where I supported the board. I thank members of the several volunteer boards of the University of Michigan business school who helped us achieve great things while I was dean. I thank members of the university boards to whom I reported: the regents of the University of Michigan who appointed me interim president and the trustees of the University of Illinois who appointed me president. I thank my colleagues on the many non-profit boards on which I have served including St. Joseph Hospital in Ann Arbor, the National Merit Scholarship Board, the American Council on Education, Argonne National Laboratory, and currently the W.E. Upjohn Institute for Employment Research. I thank my colleagues on other corporate boards of which I have been a member, especially Kelly Services and its executive chairman, Terry Adderley, and M Financial and its chairman, Peter Mullin.

You can never pay back all the people who created opportunities for you and helped you learn and grow. But you *can* pay it forward. That's why *my purpose in writing this book is to share with directors the most important things I have learned about how boards can excel.* This includes how to be a good director, how to ensure board effectiveness and how to serve as a positive influence on the organization—for profit or nonprofit—for which the board is responsible.

My goal is to help less experienced directors move rapidly down the learning curve to become effective and responsible stewards of the companies and organizations they serve. I also hope that my insights will serve as a reminder to experienced directors of things they may know but have not put into practice.

I have a broader audience in mind also. Because the boardroom is a place of privilege and privacy, most people never experience it. Yet almost everyone—investors, employees, customers, suppliers and communities—is deeply affected by what takes place there. I hope I can demystify governance and help readers understand it better.

Let me say a word about my perspective on boards. As a director and trustee, I am a governance practitioner. As an academic who teaches business and law students about boards of directors, I am a constructively critical observer. A large body of research on governance helps inform my views in both roles. I say *helps* versus *informs* because *few governance studies produce findings that a director can embrace or a professor can teach as definitive.* In this book, I will highlight a few insights that rise to this standard. But on many governance questions—such as whether the chairman and CEO roles should be filled by one person or divided between two—research findings are equivocal. Knowing this has helped motivate me to share insights from my experience so others can decide whether, when and how they apply to situations they face.

I learned at a young age that boardroom decisions are highly consequential and can affect people in deeply personal ways. I grew up in Kalamazoo, Michigan, a paper industry capital at the time. My dad was employed by a medium-sized public company, KVP-Sutherland, the product of a merger of two local family paper manufacturing businesses. As a boy, I thought that Kalamazoo was the center of the universe and KVP-Sutherland was a permanent fixture in my family's life.

One morning I woke up and discovered I was wrong. There was a new name on the main building. Brown Company had acquired KVP-Sutherland. Soon my dad left the company. Later, the Brown Company operations in Kalamazoo had yet another owner: James River Corporation. Eventually, James River closed down the entire operation and laid off everyone who worked there.

Equally stunning is the story of another public firm that everyone in Kalamazoo considered permanent: the Upjohn Company. Upjohn was a powerful, independent pharmaceutical company. The founding family was generous to the community.

In 1986, Upjohn celebrated its 100th anniversary. The chairman, Ted Parfet, a man I knew and admired, stated at the time how much he and the entire company were looking forward to Upjohn's *next* hundred years.

Nine years later, Upjohn merged with Pharmacia of Sweden, which then merged with Monsanto. The new Pharmacia focused on pharmaceuticals, retaining the G.D. Searle operations of Monsanto while shedding its agricultural businesses. Three years later, Pfizer acquired Pharmacia and all that remained of the original Upjohn Company. Today, Pfizer maintains some manufacturing activities in Kalamazoo and a veterinary medicines research group that has has been split off into Zoetis, a new public company. But employment is down drastically and the beautifully austere Upjohn corporate head-quarters, designed by Skidmore, Owings and Merrill in the 1950s, has been demolished and the site returned to its original state: an open field.

Boardroom decisions contributed to these sad outcomes for my hometown in the same way that decisions made at GFS and EQR over twenty-plus years have led—so far—to growth and prosperity. While I accept the inevitability of creative destruction in a market economy, I want boards comprised of directors who know how to maximize the prospects for success.

Boards that excel provide great governance to the organizations— companies and nonprofits—in their charge. In my experience, the bookends of great governance are high aspirations and strong results. We begin, next, with these topics.

CHAPTER 1

High Aspirations and Strong Results

The Bookends of Great Governance

What is great governance? This is a question that boards seldom ask. Perhaps directors assume the answer is obvious and everyone is on the same page. I don't think that's the case.

In this chapter, I offer my answer to that question. I make the case that the bookends, or starting and ending points, of great governance are high aspirations for and great results by the company or organization the board is overseeing.

Directors are sometimes like the stone mason who, when asked what he is doing, replies that he is constructing a wall. *Less often, they are like the mason who explains that he is building a cathedral.*

It's easy to get absorbed in the work of governance—attending committee meetings; discussing strategy, plans, and results; evaluating the CEO—and lose sight of the larger purpose of board work. There is plenty of wall construction in governance, but directors should always have an eye toward cathedral building over the long term. Asking and answering the question, "What is great governance?" can help.

Let me say a word about the importance of this question. When I was a dean at the University of Michigan, I chaired the business school's executive committee. It comprised senior faculty elected by their colleagues to advise the dean on the most consequential policy and personnel matters, especially faculty promotion and tenure decisions.

I learned many lessons in working with distinguished faculty over a decade. The most indelible of them came from Karl Weick, an eminent scholar and one of the world's great social psychologists.

"The best research begins with the best questions," Karl would remind us. Research methods are important, but what matters most is the question we are trying to answer.

"What is great governance?" is a best question for three reasons:

- *It's consequential.* A board bears final responsibility and accountability for the performance of the organization in its charge. It's popular to say that the buck stops with a senior executive—the CEO or president or managing director. But in fact, the buck ultimately stops with the board, so directors should have a clear and agreed understanding on what constitutes doing their job well.

- *It's difficult.* Is the proper measure of great governance nothing more than company or organizational performance? What are the proper performance measures? Can great governance be achieved simply by recruiting outstanding people to the board? Does the way they work together matter too? Is great governance assured if a board checks every box on good governance scorecards? If not, then what is required?

- *It's practical.* Shouldn't every board aspire to provide great governance? How can directors achieve this high aspiration without having a shared understanding of what it comprises? And don't those legislating, regulating, and evaluating governance practices need to understand the requirements of great governance?

The quality of governance is determined primarily by **results achieved** over a sustained period by the company or organization the board oversees. In the private sector in the United States, the standard measure of board performance is *economic value creation* *for owners over the long term.* In the nonprofit sector, the standard measure of board performance is *mission achievement with efficient use of resources.*

This view of governance is valid but incomplete. It is necessary but not sufficient. It fails to recognize the foundation on which value creation and mission achievement depend and the aspirations and vision they can help fulfill. It also ignores an aspiration shared by every board on which I have served: to maintain control of the organization's destiny.

My board experience has led me to a different way of thinking about the results of great governance. Value creation and mission achievement are central, but they are imbedded in the results that create them and the higher purposes they enable. A picture describes it best. I call it the Pyramid of Purpose.

Results of Great Governance: Pyramid of Purpose

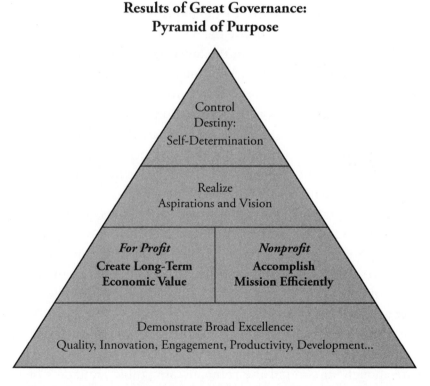

For companies, the most critical measure of board performance is *long-term economic value creation*, measured by market capitalization and total shareholder return for public companies and appraised or realized value for private companies. Return on invested capital over time is a good measure of economic value for both public and private companies. For nonprofit organizations, the most critical measure of board performance is outstanding *mission achievement* in sector-relevant ways in education, health care, human services, the arts, and so on. *Efficiency* is also important because nonprofit organizations are entrusted with resources to fulfill their missions and, usually, privileged with exemption from income taxes.

The foundation of value creation and mission achievement is *broad excellence*. This includes the company or nonprofit being admired and recognized as a leader in areas that matter such as quality, innovation, employee engagement and productivity, and leadership and people development. While no human enterprise is perfect, the customers or clients, employees, suppliers, communities, and others associated with organizations that demonstrate broad excellence value them highly. Some even love them.

That love is often based on the organization's aspirations and vision. For example, in his 2013 end-of-year statement to Apple employees, CEO Tim Cook reportedly wrote, "I am extremely proud to stand alongside you as we put innovation to work serving humankind's deepest values and highest aspirations." The best organizations provide a paycheck, of course, but they give people something more as well: purpose and ability to make a difference in the world.

Broad excellence, value creation or mission accomplishment, and achieving aspirations and vision provide the results, resources, and strength to enable the board to maintain control of the company's or nonprofit's destiny and its precious right of self-determination.

To be effective, directors must be crystal clear about the multiple purposes of the companies and organizations they oversee. Here's how we think about it at Gordon Food Service (GFS).

Start with broad excellence. For decades, John Gordon Sr. has reminded us, "Remember, our last name isn't Gordon; it's Service!" Sure enough, all around the company are visible reminders of the company's service performance: on-time deliveries, error-free orders, accident-free miles, and so on. Service excellence is part of GFS's broad excellence, which includes aggressive adoption of technology, strong employee engagement, high productivity, and development of leaders at every level. Broad excellence attracts customers and enables efficient operations, which together drive earnings—the foundation of economic value creation. Value creation enables the company to achieve its vision of providing customers the highest quality food-service products and services so they can be successful, contributing to the financial security of employees through profit-sharing and enabling the Gordon family to act on their deep Christian faith by funding missions through charitable contributions. The company's operational excellence and financial strength and its high aspirations and inspiring vision enable and motivate the board to maintain control of the company's destiny, allowing us to chart its course and maintain independence presumptively forever.

Here's an interesting illustration of the Pyramid of Purpose from the nonprofit world. Organization theorists have long been fascinated by the story of the March of Dimes. The reason is that if the sole purpose of a nonprofit organization were to achieve its mission, the March of Dimes organization would have closed up shop in the mid-1950s when its founding purpose in 1939—to combat polio as the National Foundation for Infantile Paralysis—was largely achieved with the invention of the Salk vaccine. But it didn't. Instead, leadership created a new and broader mission, one that wouldn't be so achievable! In 1958, the organization shortened its name to the National Foundation and set its sight on birth defects, arthritis, and viral disease, later narrowing its focus to prevention of birth defects, infant mortality, and premature birth.

Why did this happen? *Because nonprofit organizations and for-profit companies are about more than achieving missions or creating economic value.* They are bundles of competence and capability (at its best, broad excellence) that can be deployed to do useful things. Members and supporters become attached to these organizations because they provide structure, meaning, and relationships in their lives. The organization takes on a life of its own that can survive even beyond achievement of its mission. The leaders of these organizations, including the board, understand this, and like most of us, they are proud and independent. So directors strive to maintain control of the destiny of the organization for which they are responsible. Self-determination is success. Capitulation is failure.

In saying this, I do *not* mean to imply that every decision to sell, merge, or cease operations of a company or nonprofit is failure. For example, in 2007, Sam Zell (chairman) and the board of Equity Office Properties (EOP, a sister company to Equity Residential and at the time the largest owner of office buildings in the United States) decided to sell the company to Blackstone Group for $23 billion and Blackstone's assumption of $16 billion of debt. EOP ceased to operate as a company. This turned out to be a great governance decision by the board because 2007 was, in retrospect, the very peak of the commercial real estate market, and EOP's economic value was at an historic high. The board decided to seize that value and distribute it to shareholders. The sale of EOP was decidedly not capitulation. To the contrary, the board initiated the decision and maintained control of the company's destiny to the very end.

The four levels of the Pyramid of Purpose are interconnected and interdependent. That's why wise boards and smart senior executives strive to create a self-reinforcing, virtuous upward spiral of results across the four categories. The most challenging situation a board can face is a self-reinforcing, downward negative spiral that directors must arrest and turn around.

How does a board create a virtuous upward spiral? By setting high aspirations.

High Aspirations

Make no little plans. They have no magic to stir men's blood and probably themselves will not be realized. Make big plans; aim high in hope and work, remembering that a noble, logical diagram once recorded will never die, but long after we are gone will be a living thing, asserting itself with ever-growing insistency. Remember that our sons and grandsons are going to do things that would stagger us. Let your watchword be order and your beacon beauty. Think big.[2]

—Daniel H. Burnham, Chicago architect (1846–1912)

High aspirations are the foundation of high performance. This is as true for boards and the companies and organizations they oversee as it is for every area of human performance, team, and individual. High aspirations do not by themselves assure high performance. Execution matters too. Steve Case, founder of AOL, is reportedly fond of quoting Thomas Edison: "*Vision without execution is hallucination.*" But high aspirations are the starting point.

Burnham, the great architect of Chicago's stunning skyline and lakefront park system, had it right. Think about remarkable achievements. Here is an eclectic handful that I have observed in my lifetime:

- Landing a man on the moon and returning safely to earth
- Ending legal racial segregation in America and apartheid in South Africa
- Developing Singapore from a tiny, third-world country to an ultra-modern and prosperous city-state in thirty years
- Delivering letters and packages overnight anywhere in the United States
- Bringing together America's best college graduates and neediest kids in urban and rural classrooms
- Winning the Boston Marathon eight times in ten years
- Opening higher education—college and beyond—to people with disabilities
- Creating the iPhone

Though different in character, each of these achievements began with an aspiration that it could be, should be, *must be* done.

On May 25, 1961, in a speech before a special joint session of Congress, President John F. Kennedy set a goal of sending an American safely to the moon before the end of the decade. Eight years later, on July 20, 1969, Neil Armstrong landed on the moon and returned safely to earth.

On August 28, 1963, in a speech at the Lincoln Memorial that culminated a decade of hard work and leadership, Martin Luther

King Jr. called passionately and memorably for racial equality and an end to segregation. Less than a year later, on July 2, 1964, Congress passed the landmark Civil Rights Act of 1964. That same year, Nelson Mandela spoke of his hope for "a democratic and free society" while on trial in South Africa for his opposition to Apartheid. The system ended thirty years later with multiracial, democratic elections. Mandela, imprisoned for twenty-seven years under the old regime, was elected president.

Lee Kuan Yew led the development of modern Singapore as prime minister over three decades, from 1965 to 1990. On his watch, Singapore grew from third-world status to one of the most prosperous and modern nations in Asia. While some have criticized Lee as authoritarian and intolerant of dissent, Singapore's development in spite of its tiny landmass and lack of natural resources is a remarkable achievement and reflective of Lee's aspirations for the city-state.

While attending Yale University, Fred Smith reportedly wrote a paper for an economics class, outlining overnight delivery service in the Information Age. The paper may have received a C grade, but it was the origin of the idea that became FedEx. Today, the company has revenues in excess of $40 billion and employs 300,000 people.

In 1989, Wendy Kopp graduated from Princeton University. She did what thousands of Americans do when difficulty finding a job creates a crossroad in their lives: she became an entrepreneur. Reaching back to a paper she wrote for an undergraduate class, she began the arduous process of creating Teach for America. Since then, more than 38,000 participants have taught more than 3 million children nationwide.[3]

Jean Driscoll is an extraordinary athlete. She was born with spina bifida and grew up in Milwaukee. She was recruited to the University of Illinois to play wheelchair basketball. There, a coach, Marty Morse, spotted her as a high-potential distance athlete. The rest is history: between 1990 and 2000, Jean won the Boston Marathon, Women's Wheelchair Division, eight times in ten years.

Steve Jobs started a new company—NeXT—in the 1980s after being ousted from Apple, the company he founded, in a boardroom coup engineered by John Sculley, the man Jobs recruited from Pepsi to be Apple's CEO. (Jobs famously said, "Look, John, do you want to spend the rest of your life selling sugar water or do you want to change the world?") At an Educom conference around the same time, Sculley showed an Apple video, *The Knowledge Navigator* (watch it on YouTube). Almost twenty years later, with Jobs at the helm, Apple launched a revolutionary product: the iPhone. It was a product that no customer requested and no competitor imagined. It converted the fanciful product portrayed in *The Knowledge Navigator* into reality and supercharged the smartphone industry.

Shortly after leaving Cummins in 1987, I consulted with NeXT and had the unforgettable experience of being up close and personal with Steve Jobs. His biography by Walter Isaacson[4] captures Jobs perfectly. When it came to people-pleasing technology and amazing aesthetics, Steve *embodied* high aspirations.

I first heard the importance of high aspirations for organizations articulated by a wonderful leader, Bob Galvin, chairman of Motorola Corporation from 1959 to 1986. Bob said that the least leaders can do for their organizations is to articulate high performance aspirations. With them, he said, there's a shot at greatness. Without them, there's no chance. And leadership begins with the board.

Imagine if every board of every company and nonprofit organization in America explicitly agreed: *our aim is to provide great governance to the company or organization in our charge*. Imagine if they all understood what that commitment meant and then fulfilled it. The entire distribution of governance performance in America would shift higher. It would be a wonderful thing for companies, nonprofits, and the nation that would set an example for the world.

High Aspirations Governance: Two Examples

GFS and Governance

GFS had been around for almost ninety years when I met Paul and John Gordon in 1987. That was the year they decided to take steps to ensure quality governance, orderly management succession, and family control for generations into the future. It was not quite clear what those steps should be. Dave Gray and I helped the family identify and implement them.

GFS has been a remarkable story of growth and high performance in the ensuing twenty-five years. It has also been the story of a family dedicated to customers, employees, and service. The Gordon family practices servant leadership as a guiding principle in its stewardship of the company and expects the leaders of the company to do the same.

High Aspirations. The creation of governance arrangements for GFS was built on high aspirations for the company's future. Four stand out.

First, Paul and John wanted a governance structure that would enable the company to operate successfully for decades, even centuries, into the future—through multiple generational changes in family and management. They wanted, in other words, governance that would enable GFS to be a successful company *in perpetuity*.

We were acutely aware that few companies, public or private, achieve this goal. Corporate change and mortality statistics are sobering. Of the original companies in the Fortune 500 published in 1955, about 90 percent have disappeared from the list. This reflects the death of some companies, the absolute or relative decline of others, and the acquisition, merger, and loss of original identity of many. Few family businesses make it beyond two generations for a variety of reasons, including inadequate capital, scaling problems, failure to develop leaders, family desires for liquidity, estate taxes, and so on.

The stark reality of corporate mortality reminded us how important governance would be for GFS to have a chance to continue in perpetuity. Governance would have to anticipate and prevent or resolve all the issues that lead companies to lose control of their destinies, disappear, or die.

Second, Paul and John aspired for GFS to be a *high-performing growth company*. They wanted, somehow, to ensure the board would, every year, find the sweet spot between *stretch goals* and *acceptable risk*. This is a vital challenge for every board. Let me explain.

The board, as management's boss, must set goals, provide incentives, and monitor results to motivate high performance. Directors are also responsible for managing the enterprise's risk profile through project approvals and denials and balance sheet management. Deep financial strength is the best insurance policy against a company's becoming a mortality statistic. Excessive risk aversion leaves the organization lethargic and subject to decline and slow death (e.g., General Motors in the 1980s and 1990s). By contrast, extreme stretch goals and financial incentives can lead management to take excessive risks with crash-and-burn results (e.g., Lehman Brothers in the 2000s).

As entrepreneurial leaders of GFS, Paul and John managed this balance point personally. They constantly reinvested in the business by living modestly, thus minimizing their personal demands on company resources and enabling GFS to take prudent investment risks to expand and grow. Looking ahead to the time when the *board* would manage the balance point, they wanted to be sure the company became neither lazy and complacent nor excessively leveraged and risky.

Paul's and John's third aspiration was that GFS remain *focused on food service* and not be easily distracted by the siren song of unrelated diversification. They also preferred that the family resist the temptation to become passive investors. They understood that financial returns must be acceptable and the company would have to adopt and adapt to new technologies and circumstances. But the family had made its living for over ninety years in the food business, and they believed in its staying power. As Paul's wife, Dottie, liked to say, "It might be green beans or filet, depending on the times, but people will eat." Food service was not likely to become an obsolete industry.

Fourth, Paul and John made it clear that they wanted the company to have *strong leadership*. They understood the need for a board that expanded beyond the two of them and their sons in the business. But they had no appetite for management by committee. They emphasized the importance of a strong CEO. They also expressed the aspiration that GFS remain private, entrepreneurial, nimble, and intensely focused on customers and service even as it grew rapidly into a large and geographically far-flung enterprise.

Paul and John set high aspirations twenty-seven years ago as we wrestled with the task of creating modern governance arrangements. In summary, they sought

- a company that could survive in perpetuity;

- a high-performing growth company with stretch goals and acceptable risk;

- a company focused on food service; and

- a strongly led, entrepreneurial, service-oriented company.

Governance Structure and Philosophy. Dave Gray and I digested all this and, working closely with the Gordons, turned to the task of designing governance for GFS. We did homework on well-known and widely admired private companies, like Cargill and .S.C. Johnson, that had survived beyond a couple of generations, grown, and performed well. But mainly, we thought deeply, envisioned the future through multiple generations of continued family control, tried ideas on each other, and gradually developed an approach.

Two main elements emerged: a two-tiered governance structure and a statement of philosophy from Paul and John to future generations of family and directors. I came to think of the structure and philosophy as hardware and software, the former comprising the *what* of great governance and the latter the *how* and the *why*.

The two-tiered structure was the result of long debates about the merits of a smaller versus larger board. By small, we meant no more than five people. Remember, just two people had governed the company for decades! The great attraction of a small board was that it could act decisively and move quickly. We also expected that fewer people would mean fewer politics. We figured out, in detail, how a five-person board could be appointed and operate in a way that maintained family control while ensuring a strong family or non-family CEO and bringing in at least one outsider (i.e., neither a family member nor company employee).

But as we thought about the governance requirements of a large and growing enterprise and the need to develop younger directors while retaining the wisdom of senior members of the board, having only five directors felt too limited. We considered creating a board of up to nine people but were concerned that control of the company might become cumbersome and politicized.

For a while, we were hung up on the horns of this dilemma. Then we arrived at a solution.

We decided that the governing body that would connect to the family and exercise control of the enterprise would be a five-person *board of advisors*. GFS would have a *board of directors* of up to nine members to directly oversee the company. To avoid duplication and confusion, we empowered the board of advisors to appoint themselves as the company's board of directors with the ability to appoint up to four additional directors. We sought the benefits of a small board to represent the family and control the company and a larger board to accommodate all of the talent required to govern.

The initial GFS board of advisors was composed of Paul and John plus Paul's eldest son, Dan, Dave Gray, and me. The board of directors was composed of these five plus Paul's and John's other two sons in the business, Jim and John Gordon Jr. Paul served as chairman and John as vice chairman of both boards. There were no committees; the board handled all matters.

In an exemplary act of leadership, Paul and John soon insisted that the five-person board of advisors be composed of their three sons, Dave Gray, and me (i.e., they gave up their positions as advisors). This membership of the board of advisors has remained unchanged for twenty-five years. We are preparing now for orderly succession during the next decade.

With regard to operating philosophy—the "software" of governance—Dave and I observed early on that Paul and John had strong views about business and life. Some had direct implications for governance and leadership, such as an attitude of stewardship about the company, a philosophy of servant leadership about the people, a very cautionary approach to debt, and a belief that the family should remain focused on the industry they knew. Other things were more personal, including their deep Christian faith, its guiding influence in their lives, and their desire to devote resources to spreading God's word around the world rather than living lavishly.

As Dave and I thought about the *in perpetuity* intention for GFS, it struck us that there would be future advisors and directors who would have no idea about the thinking of these entrepreneurial owners if we didn't capture and preserve it for future dissemination. With this in mind, we asked Paul and John to write a Letter of Wishes. The title was chosen carefully. The brothers wanted their thinking to be a guide and an inspiration, not a straitjacket or set of commandments. They understood that future advisors, directors, and family members would need freedom and flexibility to make sensible decisions for their times and situations.

The Letter of Wishes makes permanent Paul's and John's high aspirations. It is a profession of their Christian faith. It addresses their views about the purpose of the company, the perpetuation and growth of the business through future generations, the role of family in the business, and the structure, financing, and focus of the company.

EQR and Governance

When Sam Zell called me in 1993 about joining the board of EQR, he made it clear that the goal was to build a great public real estate company. As the board came together and began its work, we breathed life into the aspiration Sam had articulated and came to understand what it would mean for the company and its governance.

High Aspirations. Three things defined greatness for EQR.

- First, *being a leader in creating the new, public real estate investment trust (REIT) industry*. The industry had been tarnished two decades earlier by the failure of companies with too much debt and egregious related-parties transactions (deals that benefited company insiders at the expense of other shareholders). The industry needed a reset. The liquidity crunch experienced by private real estate companies in the early 1990s encouraged or forced many to go public and provided the reset opportunity. Sam was enthusiastic about what quality public companies could mean. For shareholders, he said, they would provide liquid real estate—attractive yields in the form of dividends and capital appreciation of real estate assets with the liquidity of public company stock. For the industry, public ownership held the promise of more rational capital allocation and a reduction of the boom-and-bust development cycle that had long plagued commercial real estate.

- Second, *capitalizing on the unique window-of-opportunity in the early 1990s to acquire real estate assets at great prices.* Distressed owners and the federal government were unloading an unprecedented amount of property on the market. Sam coined a mantra for the struggling commercial real estate industry in 1991: "Stay alive 'til '95!" Meanwhile, a new public REIT could build a once-in-a-lifetime portfolio of quality real estate assets at rock-bottom prices. There were two requirements: speed and capital. From the outset, being smart, decisive, and quick to act were EQR core competencies.

- Third, *being a leader in value creation.* This would require serving residents well, operating buildings efficiently, and buying and selling properties advantageously. Central to EQR's investment thesis was that strong demand and limited supply would drive earnings and value creation.

In these three ways—leading creation of a new industry, capitalizing on a unique window of opportunity, and creating value—Sam set high aspirations for EQR and its board from its birth as a public company in 1993.

Governance Structure and Philosophy. What were the implications for governance? In terms of people, EQR needed a board composed of individuals who could quickly develop mutual respect and trust and excellent teamwork because timely decision-making was of the essence. The board required a mix of real estate professionals and people with other skills such as finance and law. From the beginning, EQR had a majority of independent trustees. As board colleague Jim

Harper told me at the time, Sam counted on EQR trustees to have real, not just technical, independence. "Joe," he said, "Sam is a force. He's smart and opinionated and no shrinking violet. He'll be counting on each of us to think independently and speak up."

Structurally, the board had a chairman (Zell) and CEO (Doug Crocker). From the outset, the board had three committees: executive, audit, and compensation. Speed combined with good judgment would require an executive committee of Sam, Doug, and independent trustees in whom the entire board had confidence to make transactional decisions between board meetings. The audit committee was charged with maintaining high credibility with capital markets. This required quality financial reporting and internal control. The compensation committee was charged with designing pay for performance (i.e., incentives for management to focus on value creation to benefit owners). The 1990s were a period of great ferment in corporate governance. Accordingly, the EQR board established a governance committee to ensure board practices in the best interests of the company's shareholders and stakeholders.

It was apparent from the outset that the EQR board would be fast company. Zell, Crocker, then-CFO (now CEO) David Neithercut, and trustees like Errol Halperin, Sheli Rosenberg, and Jim Harper were among the smartest business people I've ever met. Over the years, I would tell trustee candidates, "You need to be quick on the uptake!" There has never been room for bureaucracy on the EQR board. Detail work is done in committees. The board focuses on the big picture (strategy, risk, acquisitions, and divestitures), financial matters (operating results and the balance sheet), and the leadership team, especially the CEO. Things move fast. But when a matter is not obvious or there are differences of view, Sam as chairman slows the action to get viewpoints aired, then pushes for decisiveness. This fast company process fits EQR's business situation (multiple windows of opportunity when the combination of scale and speed is a competitive advantage) and the people around the table.

There have been many chapters in EQR's history since 1993, including its governance. The board has been as small as nine people and as large as fifteen. The company's focus within a framework of strong value creation has shifted over time: from pell-mell acquisition in the early years, to operational effectiveness, to repositioning the portfolio from garden apartments across the United States to top-quality medium- and high-rise buildings in high barrier-to-entry markets on the east and west coasts. A strong balance sheet has always been a priority. The approach to development has been conservative. There have been only a few small missteps. For example, our adventures in the furniture rental business served to remind us what our core competence is and is not.

In line with Sam's high aspirations, EQR has been a leader over the last twenty-one years in creating a vibrant public REIT industry. Today, many investment advisors recommend that REITs be part of any well-diversified portfolio. EQR's value creation has been strong. Between the initial public offering in 1993 and the end of 2013, EQR's stock has quadrupled. REITs are required to distribute at least 90 percent of their taxable income to investors, so EQR has provided a steady stream of dividends to investors during two decades of paltry interest rates on bonds and savings accounts. As Sam predicted, the modern public REIT industry has made liquid real estate a reality for investors. EQR has helped lead the way.

Conclusion

Great governance produces strong results in the form of economic value creation for companies and efficient mission achievement for nonprofits. This performance is built on a foundation of broad excellence, facilitates achievement of aspirations and vision, and enables the board to control the organization's destiny.

Great results are built on high aspirations. This is as true for companies and nonprofits as it is for individuals. The first task of the board is to set such aspirations for the enterprise and itself.

With this done, directors need to develop the proper mindset with which to oversee the company or organization in their charge. A few guiding ideas compose the stewardship thinking that underlies great governance. We turn to them next.

CHAPTER 2

Understand the Role

Stewardship Thinking

How a person approaches board service and thinks about the role of director really matters. Is there a proper metaphor to describe the job?

In my experience, the best directors think of themselves as *stewards*. They ensure careful and responsible management of the company or organization with which they have been entrusted. They are tough-minded monitors of and thoughtful advisors to those charged with managing. As representatives of owners and stakeholders, they insist on high performance and strive to grow value through prudent risk taking. As stewards, they consider matters not through the lens of self-interest but through the lens of what is best for the organization they oversee.

The metaphor of governance as stewardship yields many insights for a director. It has led me to think carefully about the privileges and responsibilities of board work. It has guided me in handling difficult situations like being a director of a failing company and managing a potential conflict of interest. It has helped me clarify what real director independence is and what director effectiveness requires. It has served as a reminder that in the leadership of organizations, there is a distinct difference between governing and managing.

I have been privileged to work with some wonderful directors. They were diligent in their work and wise in their judgments. They asked penetrating questions. They challenged management with high aspirations and stretch goals. They monitored results and rewarded high performance. They worked through knotty problems. They made tough decisions and took hard action when required. They helped renew the board by leaving when the time was right. They were great stewards.

Regrettably, I have also had experience with lesser directors. Their self-opinions were inflated. They expected to be served more than to serve. Their inattentiveness was embarrassing. Their contributions were of the Johnny and Judy one-note variety. Their disregard for boundaries undermined the chain of command. They folded in the face of conflict and controversy. They were poor stewards.

In this chapter, I share some guiding ideas for great governance—what I call *stewardship thinking*. Because I have experienced both the best and worst in governance, I know what a difference it makes when directors adopt a stewardship attitude toward their duties. The cornerstone of stewardship thinking in governance is to understand and embrace both the privileges and responsibilities of being a director.

The Privileges of Board Work

By any measure, being a director is a privilege. It's true that some people have abundant board opportunities from which to choose. But in my experience, most people are pleased and even thrilled to be invited to serve. If a primal human need is confirmation that "I'm here and I matter," an invitation to serve on the board of a good organization, for-profit or nonprofit, is one of life's confirming experiences.

Being a director includes the privileges of service, membership, protection, pay, and respect.

The Privilege of Service

We talk about "serving" on a board. Service is the mindset that directors and trustees should bring to their work. It is best described in the work of Robert Greenleaf on *Servant Leadership*.[5]

Greenleaf's view was that the best leadership begins with a desire to serve, not ambition for power, position, privilege, or prestige. Servant leadership is marked by humility, dedication, and deep recognition that what matters most is the organization and its people. Privileged positions are seductive. An attitude of servant leadership helps directors maintain proper focus in what can be a heady environment.

Servant leadership, like stewardship, reminds directors that they are not at the pinnacle of the organization; they are part of a strong base. The people of the organization do not serve the board; the board serves them. The future of the company or nonprofit is not assured with directors simply along for a prosperous ride; rather, every entity is at risk in a dynamic, competitive environment. In evaluating their own performance, directors must ask, "Has the company or organization entrusted to us thrived on our watch? Do we continue to control its destiny?"

The general concept of servant leadership is ancient. But it is associated in many people's minds with Christian beliefs, even though the New Testament and life of Christ do not appear to have been the conscious inspiration of Robert Greenleaf's work. I suspect the association is due to the revolutionary leadership example Jesus set by associating with the poor and ministering to those in need, regardless of status: "For even the Son of Man did not come to be served, but to serve, and give his life as a ransom for many."[6] Christian business leaders like the Gordons and Max DePree of Herman Miller embrace servant leadership and strive to make it a bridge between their work lives and their Christian beliefs.[7]

The Privilege of Membership

Board service is not just a group activity. It's a team sport. Membership on a board is satisfying because companies and organizations compete, and it's really fun to win.

The board is just the beginning of belonging for a director. She becomes associated with the organization and industry of which it is part. She develops networks of relationships that last for years with fellow directors and people who work with the board, including members of senior management and outside experts.

A good board bonds. Experiences over time create shared history and a collective memory of crises handled, obstacles overcome, problems solved, and goals achieved.

Does this focus on belonging imply that boards are, as some charge, clubby and incestuous, insulated and self-perpetuating? They can be. But one of the most impressive things about an effective board is its ability to manage competing values, like being simultaneously independent and collegial, critical and constructive.

Directors need both unity and occasional dissent. Too little unity and the board can't come to decisions and give clear direction to management. Too little dissent and groupthink sets in with all its perils. Too much unity and the multiple views and different takes of individual directors are lost. Too much dissent and the board dissolves into a destructive conflict.

It is important for directors and management to remember that while they all belong to the organization's leadership, their roles are distinct and different. The board governs. Management manages. The board's job in a company is primarily to represent owners. In a nonprofit, it is to represent stakeholders. Directors are obliged to monitor management with vigilance, ensuring integrity and high performance. Directors must emphatically not manage. One good description of the board's proper role is *nose in, fingers out.*

The Privilege of Protection

Directors make decisions that sometimes don't work out, such as appointing a CEO who turns out to be a dud or overpaying for an acquisition only to write down its value later. Companies can go bankrupt on a board's watch. We live in a litigious society. When things go wrong, people are encouraged to sue, and they do.

So a natural question is "At how much risk are directors?" The answer is not much, if risk means directors having to pay money out of their own pockets.

There are two reasons. One is the business judgment rule. The other is that company assets and directors and officers insurance provide resources to help satisfy successful claims against the board.

The Business Judgment Rule. A director or trustee is a *fiduciary*. A fiduciary is a person to whom property or power is entrusted for the benefit of another. As such, the director has certain duties. He or she also has protections under the law. Arguably the most important for directors is the business judgment rule.

The rule specifies that courts will not review the business decisions of directors who performed their duties

1. in good faith;

2. with the care that an ordinarily prudent person in a like position would exercise under similar circumstances; and

3. in a manner directors reasonably believe to be in the best interests of the corporation.

The business judgment rule does not necessarily protect directors from charges that they wasted corporate assets or committed fraud, misappropriation of funds, or others. Nonetheless, the rule creates a strong presumption in favor of boards, freeing members from possible liability for most decisions that result in harm to the corporation.

The business judgment rule, along with limited liability for investors and the rule of law, are key underpinnings of modern, developed economies. They facilitate pooling capital and taking risks required to develop products and services and produce and distribute them on a large scale. They allow individuals, including directors, to act in ways essential for economic development while keeping personal liability at an acceptable level.

Company Assets and Directors and Officers Insurance. Companies can indemnify their directors through provisions in their bylaws or certificates of incorporation. This means that company assets are available to defend directors in legal actions and to settle claims. In companies rich in marketable assets with conservative balance sheets, this provides a lot of protection. In companies with few tangible assets, it provides little protection. In the case of bankruptcy, it may provide no protection at all.

Directors and officers policies, commonly called D&O insurance, provide cash to cover most or all settlements or judgments in cases against directors. In large companies, such policies may be written to provide $50 to $100 million or more of coverage.

Do directors ever pay settlements out of their own pockets? Rarely but occasionally. For example, it was reported in 2005 that directors of WorldCom and Enron agreed to settlements that included personal payments.[8] Ten former outside directors of WorldCom agreed to a $54 million settlement for their roles in the company's $11 billion accounting fraud. A third, or $18 million, was paid by the directors personally with the balance paid by D&O insurance. The $18 million reportedly represented 29 percent of the directors' cumulative net worth excluding primary residences, retirement accounts, and judgment-proof joint assets. Ten former directors of Enron agreed to personally pay $13 million of a $168 million settlement for their alleged role in Enron's fraudulent accounting practices. This was 10 percent of their personal pretax profit from Enron stock sales.

These were rare exceptions to the norm of directors seldom paying settlements personally. Nonetheless, there are certain risks from which no one can indemnify a director. One is being vastly underpaid when the work of a board is most difficult, like in a crisis. Another is being sued and spending hours producing documents for plaintiffs' attorneys and testifying in depositions. And directors' reputations can suffer when things go wrong.

The Privilege of Pay (for-profit boards)

Let's be honest. A part-time job with interesting work, good colleagues, and only occasional heavy lifting that pays (in the case of corporate boards) five or six figures is an attractive proposition.

There are exceptions. For directors who are CEOs or independently wealthy, board compensation is chicken feed. When serious trouble strikes, directors would gladly return all they've earned just to make it go away.

Still, for most directors, board compensation is meaningful money, and because of the way the pay is structured, it can be a path not only to current income but also to long-term wealth building.

What do directors earn? We know with certainty what public company directors are paid because companies are required to disclose it, in detail, in their annual proxy statements. (Comprehensive data on private company board pay is not available. My impression is that it varies greatly from company to company, as do the duties of directors.) Not surprisingly, boards of the largest public companies earn much more than those of smaller companies.

These days, the value of what directors are paid depends a lot on how company stock performs. This is because most directors are paid, in part, in stock or stock options. The purpose is to focus directors, as well as management, on growing the company's earnings and enterprise value.

Surveys of public company director compensation suggest that directors are paid, on average, between $100,000 for smaller companies (those with revenues up to $500 million) and $250,000 for the largest companies. There is, however, substantial variation around mean compensation levels.

There are variations in how directors are paid. A normal arrangement is a two-part pay package. First is a base retainer plus committee fees, which can be taken in cash or deferred until retirement from the board and, until then, invested in the company's stock or, sometimes, other stock and bond funds. Second is equity-based pay, that is, restricted shares of the company's stock (restricted because shares are granted then vest over a period of time) or stock options (the right to buy company shares in the future at the price on the day of the grant).

Paying directors in stock and options is a development of the last twenty years. A fellow director, older than I, once told me that in the 1960s and '70s, directors were paid relatively nominal amounts and only in cash. In fact, he said, independent directors were forbidden or discouraged from owning stock in the companies on whose boards they served because it was considered a conflict of interest! The shareholder value revolution twenty years later changed all that. Directors owning company shares became *de rigueur* on the theory that the practice would align the board's interests with shareholders who elect them. Today the smallest public companies pay about half of director compensation in equity, and large companies pay nearly 80 percent in equity.

Another change in practice over the last twenty years is the elimination of most forms of compensation for directors beyond cash and stock. Large companies used to provide directors with pension plans and perquisites, such as the right to direct a corporate contribution to nonprofit organizations of their choice. The shareholder value movement argued, correctly in my view, that directors should not be incented to remain on the board for the purpose of accruing service that would increase their pension benefit. This could reduce director independence and impair healthy board turnover. Director-designated corporate contributions were deemed a misuse of shareholder resources because they would likely benefit the director more than the company.

The Privilege of Respect

Being respected by others is a basic human need. Respect is a central theme in film and drama.

In the great film *On the Waterfront*, Marlon Brando as Terry, laments his lost boxing career to his brother, Charley: "You don't understand. I coulda' had class. I coulda' been a contender. I coulda' been somebody!"

In the central line of Arthur Miller's great drama *Death of a Salesman*, Willie Loman's wife, Linda, cries out plaintively about her struggling husband: "Attention, attention must finally be paid to such a person!"

Being a director is being somebody. Attention is paid to directors.

The Responsibilities of Board Service

Serious responsibilities are involved in joining a board.

The proper context for understanding these responsibilities in the private sector is what academics call agency theory. The board exists to solve the *principal-agent* problem of separation of ownership and control. The owners of a public company, the shareholders, benefit from limited liability (they cannot lose more than they invest), but they need someone (an agent) to lead and manage the company on their behalf. Shareholders have ownership, but as a practical matter, most of the time management is in control. To solve the problem, shareholders elect directors to represent them. The board selects and oversees management on behalf of the owners.

The problem of competing interests between owners and managers is not theoretical. Consider this:

Interests of Owners	Interests of Managers
Maximize value	Maximize compensation
Safeguard assets	Enjoy perquisites of the job
Lead to create value	Lead to satisfy multiple stakeholders

Given competing interests, the board's responsibilities are to (1) ensure the interests of owners dominate those of management by being vigilant about the use of company resources and (2) align the interests of owners and managers through the design of incentives (pay for performance) so that management wins when, and only when, owners win.

As duly elected representatives of the company's owners, the board of directors is responsible for maximizing value over the long-term. There is long-standing debate[10] over whether the proper focus of directors is on shareholder value or stakeholders' interests. While thoughtful directors recognize and are responsive to legitimate interests of multiple stakeholders (owners, employees, customers, suppliers, communities), the cornerstone of board responsibility in the United States is to maximize shareholder value over the long term.

There is an important exception to the criterion of maximizing long-term value. When the board is considering a transaction that involves an inevitable change of control or breakup of the company, directors generally have a fiduciary duty to maximize the value of the company by considering alternative transactions and selling to the bidder offering the greatest *short-term* value. Once the sale or break-up of the company is inevitable, the board's focus turns to obtaining the most value in the short term for the company.

As fiduciaries, directors have specific legal duties. They also have professional responsibilities. These duties are similar for company and nonprofit boards.

Legal Duties

Directors have fiduciary duties of *care* and *loyalty*.

Duty of care requires that directors, in the performance of their responsibilities, exercise the care (watchfulness, attention, caution) that an ordinarily prudent person would exercise in the management of his or her own affairs under similar circumstances. Actions that do not meet this standard may be considered negligent and any damages resulting may be claimed in a lawsuit for negligence.

Directors are required to make informed business decisions by considering all material information reasonably available to them, including adequate review of key transaction documents, either by reading them or having them explained by experts.

Duty of loyalty requires that directors put the interest of the company above their own interest and that of any other organization when a conflict exists. It prohibits self-dealing by corporate directors. They may not use their position of trust and confidence to further their own interests or entrench themselves.

Professional Responsibilities

As a director, I have seldom found it difficult to exercise my duties of care and loyalty. Doing so is my natural inclination. In addition, directors receive reminders and guidance about discharging their legal duties from the board's counsel. They also have access to investment bankers, compensation consultants, and other experts.

What has proven more challenging to me and, I suspect, many directors is sorting out what my broader responsibilities are in difficult circumstances. Here are two examples.

What to do about a failing company? I was on the board of a rapidly expanding retailer. Top line growth was high due to increases in same-store sales as well as new store openings. Earnings were good and the balance sheet was leveraged but not excessively.

Then things began to go less well. Revenue growth came increasingly from new stores as same store sales stagnated. Gross margins declined as management cut prices to try to juice sales. Earnings went flat then started to decline. Cash flow was strained as a result of flat earnings and continued expansion. I found myself paying close attention and feeling concerned. I extrapolated trends. I didn't like where things were going.

During this time, management tried to be reassuring. But in the process of what psychologists call sense-making, that is, figuring out what various bits of information might mean, four things occurred in close succession that unnerved me.

First, the very talented president and CEO of the company resigned and took a bigger and better job elsewhere. I thought we should appoint an interim and do a search for his successor. The rest of the board was comfortable with an internal promotion and felt that an interim title would signal weak support and failure would be a self-fulfilling prophecy.

Second, one of the directors pointed out in a board meeting especially poor performance of one of our stores and asked management for an explanation. The new CEO said, "A Walmart opened down the street and that hurt us. But I've competed against Walmart; if we hang in there, they'll let up." I thought this was the dumbest assertion I'd ever heard in a business meeting. I challenged it. The executive softened his stance but only a little.

Third, we did a tour of the company's distribution center. The purpose was to show off the inventory management system, but what I noticed was poor housekeeping. There were boxes in aisles, open

cartons, and a general sense of disarray. Soon after, my dad was looking for a particular product that I was sure would be carried in one
of the company's stores because we were a category killer retailer. We
went shopping. Sure enough, the store carried it, but that day it was
stocked-out. My dad wasn't impressed, and I was embarrassed.

Fourth, we decided to borrow money because earnings were stag-
nant, the balance sheet was strained, and growth was chewing up
cash. Management told the board what the interest rate would likely
be, and we deemed it acceptable. I'll never forget learning soon after
the bond offering that the final rate was more than a third higher
than we had expected—a junk bond rate! I was shocked. The public
debt market was telling us something very different about the risk
profile and credit worthiness of the company than we were hearing
from management.

I sat down over a weekend and thought about what I had been
experiencing. Something about it seemed familiar. Then I remem-
bered a presentation by John Hackett, the brilliant chief financial
officer of Cummins, I had heard a decade earlier. His title was "How
Companies Fail." It was a "stages" approach, like Gail Sheehy's life
phases in *Passages* or Elisabeth Kubler-Ross's process of grief in
On Death and Dying. I was stunned to realize, based on Hackett's
stages of how companies fail, that I was a director of a company mid-
way through a process that could result in bankruptcy.

The question was what to do? This was a difficult situation for
a director. I had legal duties of care and loyalty and the protection
of the business judgment rule. But I was deeply concerned about
the company's prospects. Financial failure would be the antithesis
of my responsibility as a fiduciary, deeply harmful to shareholders
and stakeholders alike. But in conversation, I found that others on
the board were not nearly as concerned as I, and management was
relentlessly reassuring.

I had a great desire to flee. I felt like a passenger on the Titanic
who was convinced we'd hit an iceberg and were likely to go down
while everyone around me was still enjoying dinner and dancing.
Resigning from the board was an option, of course, because directors
can do so at any time and are not obliged to provide an explanation.

But it seemed to me that cutting and running without making the best case possible to my board colleagues as to what I believed was happening and, more important, *what actions needed to occur to rescue the situation* would be irresponsible.

So I put together a short presentation and shared it with the chairman and independent directors. It included five actions the company had to take for me to continue in good conscience as a director: conserving cash, halting new store openings, closing money-losing stores, discontinuing a related diversification, and evaluating whether we had the right CEO or needed to recruit one fully up to the difficult job facing us.

The board discussed my analysis and recommendation. They disagreed. I resigned. Eighteen months later, the company declared bankruptcy.

I took no pleasure in it, and I don't intend this as an "I told you so" tale. Rather, it is a story of the real nature of a director's responsibility in a difficult business situation. Absent extreme good luck, most directors will experience some failures because pursuing returns for shareholders involves risk. I've always liked my dad's notion that in tough situations your conduct has to allow you to look yourself in the mirror in the morning. That's a good standard to guide a director in a tough spot.

What to do about a possible conflict of interest? Directors have to be attuned to potential conflicts of interest when they consider joining or remaining on a board. They must honor their duty of loyalty to the company if push comes to shove. And independent directors must be prepared to challenge the prevailing wisdom, including backing up conviction with resignation if necessary.

It would be nice if conflicts were all crystal clear. Then deciding how to handle them would be easy. But they're not. I had an experience that illustrates the point. The story is short because my board service lasted exactly one meeting.

It occurred while I was dean of the business school at the University of Michigan. I became acquainted with Sam Wyly, one of our graduates. Sam was a successful, colorful, and sometimes controversial Texas entrepreneur. We had several meetings. Sam visited the school, and I ultimately asked him to consider a $10 million gift to fund half the cost of constructing a much-needed new building on campus. Through this process, we got to know each other, and Sam invited me to join the board of a public company, Sterling Software, of which he was chairman. He and his brother Charles were major investors.

I engaged in careful due diligence and determined that the company was solid and had a good reputation. I was confident in my ability to be independent in thought and action as a director because that's my makeup. (Like most university professors, I am skeptical of authority and don't like anyone telling me what to do.) So I joined the board.

I thought things would be fine until I attended my first meeting. There, I was surprised to find myself thinking and feeling uncomfortable about the concurrent timing of Sam's major gift to the school and my joining the board as an independent director of a public company he chaired. Could I be as independent as I naturally was? With Sam, his brother, and his son all on the board, I wasn't sure I could. I decided to play it safe and never find out. I went to Sam after the meeting and told him I was concerned that I could find myself in a conflict between my roles as dean of the business school to which he was a donor and an independent director. Out of an abundance of caution, I had decided it would be best for me not to serve on the board. Sam was gracious, and that was the end of it. It was a decision that cost me a lot of money—several million dollars in light of stock and options and the later sale of the company—but it passed the "look yourself in the mirror" standard.

The Rise of the Independent Directors

Independent directors now dominate the boards of public companies, holding over 80 percent of board seats. Only independent directors can serve on three key committees: audit, compensation, and governance.

An independent director can only fulfill her duties—legal and practical—if she resolves to be truly independent as well as candid and constructive.

Independent. Corporate boards used to be composed mainly of company executives and professionals who served them, such as bankers and attorneys. This was good in terms of directors' knowledge of the company and their ability to come to agreement and get things done. It was often not good in terms of directors putting their own interests (jobs, compensation, and benefits for inside directors, professional work and related fees for outside directors) above those of shareholders. It also hindered tough-minded monitoring and dismissal of underperforming CEOs. Relationships were too cozy and reciprocal.

The shareholder value revolution of the 1980s had profound consequences for board focus, size, and composition. Total shareholder return (share price plus dividends) became a key measure of board performance and effectiveness. A vigorous market for corporate control was reflected in acquisition and merger activity.

As a result, the human makeup of boards changed dramatically. Independent directors came to dominate public company boards. Boards became smaller: nine to twelve directors is customary now instead of fifteen or more. The chairman and CEO roles, previously united, are now frequently divided. The board's agenda, once the exclusive domain of the chairman/CEO, is now set in consultation with a lead independent director. Executive sessions of the independent directors occur regularly whereas previously they were rare and almost always signaled that the CEO was in trouble. Board compensation is now substantial because independent directors are no longer paid indirectly through legal and consulting fees and banking relationships.

The rise of independent directors has created an important question: What does *independence* really mean? It's useful to draw a distinction between *technical* independence and *real* independence. Technical independence, as required by the SEC and stock exchange listing standards, increases the odds of, but does not ensure, real independence.

In my experience, real independence is rooted in a director's attitude and state of mind combined with a willingness to speak up and, if required, act in ways not in one's immediate self-interest.

Independence requires a director to

- *be curious,* with a big appetite for facts, concepts, insights, ideas, and people from whom the director can learn so that independent thinking is well-informed;

- *question and challenge,* especially traditional practices, conventional wisdom, and majority views;

- *trust but verify,* one of President Ronald Reagan's favorite phrases;

- *have perspective* that puts current issues and events in context: past and future, related matters, and relative importance. This is sometimes called the helicopter view; and

- *be creative,* offering novel and innovative solutions to problems with which the board and management are wrestling.

Hallmarks of independent behavior are

- *asking questions* more than broadcasting;

- *drilling down* when warranted;

- *precipitating conflict* when required;

- *tolerating discomfort;*

- *speaking truth to power;*

- *searching for common ground* and solutions around which the board can unite; and

- *resigning from the board* if legal and professional duties or the dictates of conscience cannot be fulfilled.

The independence of a director is of little value unless it is combined with two others qualities: candor and constructiveness.

Candor. Candor is a fiduciary duty in addition to care and loyalty.

Directors are selected for their judgment, above all. The board, senior management, and the company only benefit if directors are candid, that is, speak out honestly about what is on their minds. They call things as they see them. They raise questions, including uncomfortable ones.

Of course, directors have to be selective. Is the issue worth addressing? Has someone else already made the point? Are they talking just to hear themselves speak? The most valued directors listen a lot and speak selectively. It's important to protect the value of your verbal currency.

Being candid sounds easy, but it's not. I served on the board of a small, family-owned company with a long history. The family CEO had done a good job with the company on his watch. But it was a difficult, cyclical business, and he had weathered several recessions with requisite cost cutting, including layoffs—always a difficult task.

One day I got a call at the office. I could hear the emotional distress in the CEO's voice. "I have to see you," he said. "I want to sell the company. I'm talking with each director."

I was shocked. There had been no warning of this, and the company had been in existence for many decades. I agreed to meet with him that afternoon.

When he walked in, I could see the stress on his face. He saw bad times coming and did not—*did not*—want to be at the helm through another recession. He had put out some feelers and found a buyer willing to purchase the company for a particular sum. He asked what I thought.

The answer he was looking for was obvious. He was seeking support to do what he desperately wanted to do. Providing it would have been easy. I had no ownership stake in the company, I served as a director at his and the family's pleasure, and the modest directors' fees were of no great consequence to me.

Yet with several hours to consider the matter, I had decided what I thought and was candid with the CEO:

> I understand. I had to lay people off at Cummins, and it was the hardest thing I've ever done professionally. So I empathize. But I cannot in good conscience advise you to sell the company or support your doing so. This is a family business built over generations. I believe its market value is exceptionally low right now because you're

not the only one who believes a recession is coming. A fire sale of the company today at a low point in its value would be wrong—for you and the family. I urge you to lead the company through this downturn and use the time to fix everything that will increase its value when volume returns. Then, reconsider whether to sell the company at a value that reflects the work that you, your father, and others have done over so many years to make it what it is today.

The CEO was disappointed and disagreed. We all like to hear what we want to hear, not necessarily what we need to hear. One of a director's most important duties is to be candid and honest, especially when doing so challenges a consequential direction that management or the board wants to pursue but with which the director disagrees.

The end of this particular story is a good one. Other directors expressed views similar to mine. The CEO led through the recession. Three years later, revenues and profits were strong, and he sold the company with the full support of the board and family for *four times* what he had been offered just thirty-six months earlier. That's the difference directors can make at a critical time in a company's and an executive's life. Candor is required, even if it is uncomfortable or inconvenient.

Constructiveness. I have found there is a big difference between quality academic research and successful leadership and management. In their search for truth, faculty must be analytical and *deconstruct* what they examine. Leaders and managers should be analytical, but they must also take *constructive* action in order to create value and move their organizations forward.

I have enormous respect for the scientific method and the value it brings to a world drawn to fashion, fads, false correlations, and fatuous theories. But I also deeply appreciate that leaders and managers must go beyond analysis and understanding to action and results.

This is the reason for a culture gap between academics and leaders/managers. Academics are inclined to be skeptical of leadership slogans such as "The Way Forward," a recent theme and name of a restructuring plan at Ford Motor Company. They can also be skeptical of their colleagues whose work appears to be longer on inspiration than evidence.

The need for constructive action is why I sometimes say to executives considering a change, "Remember, you need to be right twice!" It's usually not hard to figure out what you want to *stop* doing when a person or course of action isn't working out. The harder part is figuring out what to do *next*, such as recruiting the right person or embarking on a new strategy.

Good directors understand this. So they push themselves when opining on a situation about which they are concerned to share not only their analysis but also what might be done to make things better. As a director, when I'm concerned but can't come up with good alternatives, I will simply describe the communication of my concern as "sharing agony" and admit I don't know what to do about it. This is better than either of the alternatives—worrying in silence or offering a lame suggestion in which I'm not confident.

Leading the Company: Governing versus Managing

Directors must wrap their minds around the role of the board versus the role of senior management in leading the company.

It's challenging because while the board has ultimate *accountability* for company performance, it is definitely not the board's job to *manage* the company.

One governance reform that has been suggested is making directorships full-time jobs to level the playing field between senior management and the boards to which they are accountable. This is a terrible idea. There are sound reasons that the CEO reports to a board of able, committed part timers versus full timers.

The CEO reporting to a group ensures that multiple points of view and time for deliberation will be reflected in major decisions. This is not a guarantee against reflexive, impulsive, and occasionally catastrophic decisions, but it helps.

The board being part-time reduces the odds of ambiguity and confusion over who is in charge. Unity of command is the principle that no one in an organization should report to more than one person. It may seem a little quaint and antiquated in a world of matrix structures and network organizations, but it is essential at the most senior level. People must understand that the board appoints the CEO, the CEO reports to the board, and everyone else reports directly or ultimately to the CEO.

Take my word on this. It's based not only on sound management theory but also on my own hard-won and unhappy experience. In one of my jobs reporting to a board, several board members developed the habit of going directly to one of my subordinates to get what they wanted. Neither they nor he informed me. It ended badly, as such things usually do.

The board's being part-time does not guarantee unity of command, but it helps reduce the potential for directors to compete with senior management over who performs executive and operational functions of leadership. The executive function of management is to execute policy, direction, and decisions that, at a high level, are made by the board, usually on management's recommendation. The operational function of management is to operate the company on a day-to-day basis, fulfilling the organization's mission, doing its business, and attending to myriad details. Neither the executive nor operational function is the work of the board.

What, then, is the board's work? In a word, it's *governance*.

In later chapters, I will discuss in detail what constitutes the substance and process of great governance. Suffice it to say that governance involves four key functions of the board:

1. Appointing, incenting, evaluating, and, when necessary, removing the CEO and senior management.

2. Setting aspirations and direction and approving strategy and policy, plans, (annual and long-range) and performance measurements. This includes making the most consequential decisions that define the entity's

   • risk profile (strategic bets and capital structure);

- culture (tone at the top, beliefs, values, style); and
- future (major initiatives, capital investments, mergers and acquisitions).

3. Monitoring results and verifying the integrity and accuracy of disclosure, especially of financial condition and results.

4. Self-monitoring and renewal of the board.

When the board performs these functions well, it enables senior management to lead the company effectively and facilitates the work of the organization.

A different take on governance, wholly consistent with these four functions, involves a paradox, one that seems little understood by many governance reformers. The board has two responsibilities vis-à-vis management:

- *Monitoring and holding management accountable* for performance and results
- *Supporting and helping management succeed* in achieving high performance and intended results

There is nothing novel about the coexistence of these functions. They can appear contradictory but don't need to be. Parents face a similar challenge. We have to expect a lot of our kids, monitor their behavior and performance, and ensure proper consequences. We also need to support, advise, and occasionally reassure them as they face new challenges, difficult situations, and trying circumstances. *Tough love* comes to mind.

Done well, the board's performance of these dual roles has complete *integrity*, in the purest sense of the word. They are performed seamlessly and are mutually reinforcing. They engender respect.

They can be done wrong, however. I remember a director whose day job involved doing depositions; his style was skeptical and intimidating. He had the same style as a board member interacting with management. I also remember a director whose transparent need for acceptance and affection made her incapable of asking hard questions or being straight with management about performance failures.

Her questions were all softballs, and her evaluative comments about management were relentlessly complimentary.

Like the best parents, good directors know that monitoring and disciplining are necessary but not sufficient conditions for growth, development, and high performance. The same is true of help and support. A rich mix of both is essential.

Boards in a Goldfish Bowl

Corporate (and to a lesser degree nonprofit) directors function in a charged environment these days. More than ever, directors are held accountable for performance. Shareholders and stakeholders expect the board to attend to their many, often competing, interests, claims, and concerns.

Boards are under increased surveillance because of highly visible calamities that have befallen some companies. Think Lehman Brothers and General Motors. Over and over, the question has arisen: Where were the boards?

Investors and the public are understandably skeptical about the attentiveness and effectiveness of boards, especially in light of the power, privilege, and rewards their members enjoy. The authors of a recent book titled *Money for Nothing: How the Failure of Corporate Boards is Ruining American Business and Costing Us Trillions*[11] are unrestrained in their indictment of directors. From inattentiveness to excessive executive compensation, their criticisms are relentless.

Yet there is no shortage of institutions and individuals setting ground rules for boards, looking over directors' shoulders and advising or urging governance reform. A short list would include traditional parties like Congress, the SEC, and stock exchanges and more recent entries like proxy advisory services and activist investors.

Proxy advisory services such as ISS and Glass Lewis analyze companies' annual proxy statements and governance practices and advise institutional investors on how to vote their shares. Matters include director elections, executive compensation, and various initiatives put forth by management and investors who qualify for proxy access.

These services have become quite powerful because their advice is influential on voting outcomes.

Also influential are activist shareholders such as Bill Ackman, Daniel Loeb, Nelson Peltz, and Carl Icahn and the investment vehicles they control. Institutional investors are also a powerful force. They target boards and companies for change, sometimes on their own, sometimes in partnership with activists. The largest of them, such as Blackrock, Calpers, and TIAA-CREF take an interest in governance because their size does not permit them to do the "Wall Street Walk"—that is, sell shares if they disagree with the company. Others, such as union pension funds and religious orders, choose to stand and fight on principle rather than sell and exit.

In short, boards may meet in private, but they live in a goldfish bowl.

Conclusion

Great governance requires directors who understand the role of the board. Governance is best thought of as stewardship.

Directors should know and embrace their responsibilities as they enjoy their privileges. The best directors are independent in the deepest sense—attentive, curious, challenging, and unafraid to take action when required. They monitor management and hold them accountable while providing help and support.

Effective stewardship requires a deep understanding of the entity being governed. This is the subject to which we turn next.

CHAPTER 3

Understand the Enterprise

What Is a Company (School, Hospital ...)?

The first marketing course I took began with an assignment to read "A Note on the Worldwide Watch Industry," a dense document describing the global market for watches including market participants, products, price points, volumes, and distribution channels.

My section mates and I went to class expecting a discussion of the watch industry. That didn't happen. Instead, our professor, Steve Starr, faced the class and asked a simple question: "What is a watch?"

The answer turned out to be anything but simple.

A watch is a way of keeping time and doing so portably. As a young man, this was the only way I had ever thought about watches.

But, as various students pointed out, a watch can be many things, including a piece of jewelry, a fashion accessory, an expression of personal values and taste, a work of art, a collector's item, a store of value, a talisman, a gift with significance and meaning, a status symbol, a family heirloom, and more. "What is a watch?" turned out to be the best possible introduction to the subject of marketing.

There is a similar question that corporate directors should ask themselves: What is a company? And nonprofit directors should ask, "What is a hospital or university or school?" It is impossible to be an effective steward of an entity unless you deeply understand its character. Let me illustrate by focusing on *what is a company?*

The standard definition is that a company is a business firm or enterprise. This is true but not very useful. In my experience, a company is many things to many people. The deeper answer is rich, complex, and consequential for directors.

In the following sections, I describe what I think a company is and some implications for governance. In addition to being a business enterprise, a company is

- a legal entity
- an economic entity
- a human community
- a story
- a means as well as an end
- an open system

A Legal Entity

While the birth of a company involves entrepreneurial effort and risk taking, the actual creation of the company is a legal matter. Once entrepreneurs decide that the time has come to put formality and ownership around their work, they can choose from a variety of legal structures including corporations, S-corporations, benefit corporations, limited liability companies, sole proprietorships, and partnerships. We will primarily focus on corporations because most (though not all) companies that have boards of directors are incorporated.

Corporations are chartered by states, a throwback to the centuries when the English crown, wishing to achieve certain goals for the nation but not wishing to risk its own capital, chartered companies. The first was the East India Company, granted a Royal Charter by Elizabeth I on December 31, 1600, for the purpose of fostering trade with India.

It is hard to overstate the ingenuity and effectiveness of the corporate form of organization. Without it, large-scale deployment of new technology (e.g., canals in the eighteenth century, railroads in the nineteenth century, and automobiles, airplanes, and airlines in the twentieth) would have been impossible. Shares of ownership and their dividends and growth in value incented people to invest their savings in these companies. Limited liability ensured they could lose no more than they invested. The former appealed to people's animal spirits and encouraged them to take risk. The latter helped assuage their fear of loss and helped protect them from personal financial catastrophe.

Ownership is important to directors because boards are accountable to the owners of public companies who elect them and private companies who select them. While there is substantial overlap in the duties of directors of public and private companies, there are also important differences.

Private Companies. In America, private companies are far more numerous than public, even though you would think just the opposite if you only read about business in the *Wall Street Journal* and *New York Times*. While there are 15,000 publicly traded companies in the United States, a third of which trade on exchanges, there are 27 million private firms, of which 5.7 million have employees.[12]

A private company, whatever its legal structure—corporate, sole proprietorship, partnership, limited liability company—is owned by one or more individuals. The owners take the risks and call the shots.

Many private companies are multi-generational family businesses. Some are enormous like Cargill and Koch Industries. Others are large, like Gordon Food Service. Most are small. For many families, the business is not only a source of employment and wealth but also a projection of family values and a point of pride. Given human nature, the family business can also be a catalyst for conflict.

Family-owned and -controlled businesses are not the only private companies in America. Private equity is an important owner. Governance in this case is simple. The private equity firm installs the management and calls the shots, sometimes with a handpicked board, sometimes with no board at all. My focus is not on these situations but on private companies that are owned or controlled by a family or some other group that chooses to create a board to which management is accountable.

In my years of fundraising as a dean and president, I met many corporate executives. I found that few private business owners wished their companies were public, while many public company executives quietly envied the advantages of their private company peers. Private companies are typically taken public to secure access to capital for growth, to establish a market for the company's stock for estate-planning purposes, and to satisfy the liquidity and financial diversification desires of family members. These are powerful reasons for going public. But there is a lot of baggage in being a public company including governance, reporting, and compliance requirements.

Some, but not all, private companies choose to have formal governance—that is, a board of directors or a family council that serves as a quasi-board. In small companies, the owner usually runs the business. Period. As a company grows, the owner must choose whether or not to create a governance structure. The default is *not*. There's a lot to be said for not creating a governance structure, such as untrammeled freedom and no relationships to manage with overseers and advisors.

Why, then, do the owners of many private companies choose to create a board of directors and—let's be honest—subject themselves to it? My experience with Gordon Food Service is instructive in this regard.

When I met Paul and John in 1987, they said they thought it would benefit the company over the long term to have a more formal board with outside directors. They were facing generational succession—from themselves to their sons and others—in senior management. They were also interested in creating durable ownership and control arrangements for the company that would enable it to continue in perpetuity. They thought that outside directors might be helpful in meeting these challenges.

I remember well my first meeting with Paul and John in Grand Rapids. It was on Black Monday, October 19, 1987, when the Dow Jones Industrial Average dropped 508 points, or 22 percent.

It was a striking experience to be with the Gordons that afternoon as their assistant provided occasional updates on the market mayhem. They seemed interested but not particularly concerned. Our meeting continued without a hitch. The Gordons' connection to the stock market was (and is) dramatically less than that of public companies and their executives.

The financial performance of GFS is measured on revenue, earnings, cash flow, and return on assets and investment, not stock price. The Gordons do not look to the equity markets as a source of capital, preferring to fund the business internally and with conservative, secured borrowing. Other things being equal, they would rather have the market high than low because it affects the value of investments in the employee' profit-sharing plan and the general mood of the economy. But it's far from life-or-death with them.

I believe that the Gordons, like many private business owners, feel more in control of their destiny than do most public company executives. They probably are. With only the family and a board they created to whom to be accountable and without quarterly public reporting of results and an ever-fluctuating share price, they can take the long view in making decisions about what's best for their customers and the company. They really like it that way. In my experience, so do most private owners.

A variation on private company ownership is the ESOP (Employee Stock Ownership Plan). While public companies can have ESOPs, they are more often found in closely held private companies where they can be used to buy part or all of the shares of existing owners. The ESOP is a type of employee benefit plan that buys and holds company stock for the benefit of a broad group of employees. Federal law provides significant tax advantages. Private companies with ESOPs have special governance considerations including proper representation of employee interests. The National Center for Employee Ownership is an excellent resource for all aspects of ESOPs, including governance.

Controlled Public Companies. This is a special category of public company that retains aspects of private ownership while creating the opportunity for public ownership of shares. Some of America's best-known companies, including Berkshire Hathaway, Dreamworks, Facebook, Ford, Google, Hershey, and the New York Times are controlled public companies. I've been a director for some time of such a company, Kelly Services, which is controlled by Terence Adderley and his family.

In 2005, the New York Stock Exchange defined controlled companies as those in which more "more than 50 percent of the voting power is held by an individual, group [often a family], or another company" and "which is therefore exempt from the director independence requirements for the board, nominating/corporate governance committee and compensation committee."[13]

Such companies represent an effort to achieve the best of public and private company ownership. The public aspect provides access to capital, liquidity, and estate planning and diversification benefits to controlling shareholders. It also creates the opportunity for other shareholders to take what they hope will be a profitable ride with the controlling shareholders at the wheel. The controlled aspect can to a degree insulate the company from certain public company pressures that, some say, involve short-termism (e.g., to achieve quarterly earnings goals) and serious distractions (e.g., unwelcome takeover bids).

A controlled public company is something of a compromise between public and private. There are, of course, downsides to any compromise. Critics of this ownership structure,[14] which is often achieved through a dual class share structure (one class with voting privileges, the other without), believe that conflict of interest is inherent in controlled public company ownership. They worry that the interests of minority shareholders can be subjugated to the interests of those in control and that absence of opportunity for takeover without the consent of the controlling shareholders reduces the value of shares for owners. The view of controlling shareholder tends to be (though stated more politely than this) "if you don't like the arrangement, don't buy the shares."

In terms of governance, directors of controlled public companies have three key responsibilities in addition to those shared by all public company directors: (1) to advise the controlling shareholder(s), (2) to plan for orderly transition of ownership and management, and (3) to ensure proper representation and fair treatment of all shareholders, including those in the minority and without a vote. This means, among other things, being attentive to what are called related parties transactions—that is, contracts, deals, and other arrangements between the company and controlling shareholders and their friends and relatives. An example would be the company leasing office space from a controlling shareholder. Directors need to ensure that there is no sweetheart deal that enriches the controlling shareholder at the expense of others. Due diligence on the part of directors would include requiring that the lease be based on market rates.

Warren Buffett and his long-time partner, Charlie Munger, have offered a spirited defense of controlled public company governance, specifically of Berkshire Hathaway. This has taken the form of caustic criticism of the performance of some other public company boards and some governance reforms advocated by activists, Congress, and the S.E.C.

Here is Buffett speaking about the Berkshire board:

> We have real owners on our board. What they make for being board members is really inconsequential … compared to their investment. They are friends of mine. They are smart. They are very smart. I mean they are handpicked in terms of business brain power and quality of human being. I really think that we have the best board in the country. But for the people that make their evaluations by check lists, either in terms of diversity or in terms of supposed independence (although I don't know how anybody that is getting half of their income from board memberships can be independent) we may not stack up so well. But … there is no group of people I would rather have in charge of the decision subsequent to my death [as to who my successor will be] than the people that we have got on our board.[15]

Here is Munger speaking on governance reform:

> A lot of people think that we'll fix our corporate governance problems by making the corporate directors have more power, kind of like the justices of a typical Supreme Court, or the council members of a typical city. But a Supreme Court makes a hundred decisions a year … very pompously and slowly, and a typical city council are people up there posturing, playing to one group or another. It's a disastrous system of governance … we don't want those systems in our corporations.[16]

Berkshire Hathaway's great financial performance insulates it from effective criticism of its governance practices. As a general case, I think it's desirable for controlled public company boards to comprise mainly directors whose stature and independence would make them welcome on any board.

Public Companies. When people think about corporate governance and boards of directors, they usually have in mind public companies with broad ownership and no controlling shareholder. This is where the agency problem of separation of ownership and control is most obvious and a competent, effective board of directors to represent shareholders and appoint, monitor, and assist management is the solution.

EQR is such a company. EQR is the United States' largest multi-family real estate investment trust. Sam Zell, the chairman, has a significant holding of EQR stock—about 3.2 percent, or over 10 million shares. But neither he nor any other shareholder has a controlling interest.

EQR, like other non-controlled companies, is truly public in the sense that there is only one class of common stock, and every share has an identical voting right. No shareholder has the ultimate or determining say on any matter, including the election of the board of trustees, appointment of the CEO, or whether to accept or reject a tender offer for the entire company. Shareholders elect the board annually on a one-share-one-vote basis, and the board has authority over most key corporate decisions on a majority rule basis.

Ownership in large public companies like EQR is broadly distributed across institutional and individual investors. EQR has thousands of shareholders. Institutions, including mutual fund companies such as Fidelity and Vanguard and pension funds such as TIAA-CREF and Calpers, own large blocks of EQR on behalf of millions of investors and beneficiaries. Individual shareholders in EQR range from those with large holdings, like Zell, to mom and pop investors who may own only a few, or a few hundred, shares. The board of trustees represents them all.

In the case of private companies with boards of directors and controlled public companies which must have boards, the answer to the question of who selects or elects directors is obvious: the private owner(s) or controlling shareholder(s). In the case of public companies, the answer is not so obvious. Who decides who will be slated for election? And among the directors elected, who will lead the board?

Traditionally, the answer to these questions was that one individual, serving as both chairman of the board and chief executive officer of the company, played the dominant role in selecting board nominees and running the show. Sometimes this worked extremely well. There is a lot to be said for having a strong leader and a minimum of organizational ambiguity (e.g., Warren Buffett at Berkshire Hathaway for the last forty-plus years). But it has not always worked well and has sometimes led to disastrous results (e.g., WorldCom, Tyco, and other infamous implosions associated with a dominant chairman and CEO and a pliable board).

The result has been substantial reform in how directors are slated for nomination and how boards are structured and operate. In the past, the chairman/CEO played a key role in board elections. Today, a governance committee of independent directors plays that role. In the past, separating the chairman and CEO role was rare; today it is quite common. In the past, the chairman/CEO set the agenda and ran the meetings. Today, there is usually a lead independent director who works with the chairman to set the agenda and run regularly scheduled executive sessions of the independent directors. In the past, there were often a number of company executives on the board. Today, there is usually only one, the CEO. As a result—and as required by listing exchanges—independent directors dominate public company boards and only they serve on key committees including audit, compensation and governance.

An Economic Entity

To take off, survive, and thrive, a company's economics must work. There must be enough demand for its products and services to generate revenue to cover costs, expenses, and other obligations. The company must operate efficiently enough to enable it to compete successfully on price, quality, and service. To attract essential capital, the company must, over time, earn a competitive return on investment.

For directors, the company as an economic entity is a cornerstone assumption in governance. There is nothing worse than directors who don't understand basic economics. They are the equivalent of drivers without drivers' training. They shouldn't be behind the wheel.

Of all the principles of economics, the most important is supply and demand. When something is in short supply and demand is high, its price and value go up. When something is abundantly supplied and demand is low, its price and value go down

My years on the board of EQR have instilled in me the importance of directors looking at business through the lens of supply and demand. Sam Zell likes to say that competition is a great thing—for the other guy! Limited supply makes things dearer and positions a company to be more profitable.

Supply and Demand in Action. Let me offer an example of supply and demand as it has played out at EQR, much to the advantage of our shareholders. It is the story of repositioning EQR's portfolio of apartment buildings into high barrier to entry markets across the nation.

EQR was created as a public company in 1993 to provide an infusion of growth capital into Sam Zell's privately owned apartment business along with a portfolio of properties provided by a company named Starwood and its founder, a brilliant real estate entrepreneur named Barry Sternlicht. The recession had deeply depressed demand for and, therefore, prices of apartment properties across the country. In addition, the Federal Deposit Insurance Corporation was making available for sale properties that it owned as a result of the savings and loan crisis. Capitalizing on these opportunities, EQR tapped the public debt and equity markets and went on an aggressive, multi-year buying spree, acquiring quality garden apartment properties across the nation from motivated sellers at bargain basement prices.

A decade later, EQR was humming. Demand for apartments had rebounded. Occupancy levels and rents had risen, substantially increasing the value of the properties EQR purchased in the 1990s. After careful consideration of the future of supply and demand for apartments, the board, on management's recommendation, made a strategic decision to reposition EQR's entire portfolio. We sold much of what we owned, exiting certain geographical markets where we forecast too little demand or too much new supply and bought properties in markets where we forecast high demand for apartments and little new supply. Our catch phrase for the demand side of the equation was that EQR would be "where people want to live, work, and play." The catch phrase for low supply conditions was "high barrier to entry markets." We bought and developed properties in densely populated, desirable urban areas, primarily on the east and west coasts, with low land availability and strenuous permitting conditions for building new properties. Think Boston, New York, Washington, San Francisco, and Seattle.

The repositioning strategy—which completely changed EQR's property portfolio—was entirely driven by considerations of supply and demand.

Financial Statement Analysis. A company's economic health is measured primarily with financial data. This brings us to the issue of financial literacy and the importance of having one or more financial experts on the board.

The terms *financial literacy* and *financial experts* are not randomly chosen. Stock exchange listing standards (the requirements companies must meet to be listed and have their shares traded on the exchange) use them to specify the level of financial knowledge directors must have to serve on the board's audit committee.

For example, the listing standards of the New York Stock Exchange state that each member of the audit committee must be financially literate, as such qualification is determined by the board in its business judgment. The standards also require that at least one member of the company must have "accounting or related financial management expertise." This requirement relates to Section 407 of the Sarbanes-Oxley Act of 2002, which requires public companies to disclose whether their audit committees include at least one member who is an "audit committee financial expert." The SEC defines a financial expert as a person with all of the following attributes:

- An understanding of generally accepted accounting principles and financial statements
- The ability to assess the general application of such principles in connection with the accounting for estimates, accruals, and reserves
- Experience preparing, auditing, analyzing, or evaluating financial statements or actively supervising one or more persons engaged in such activities
- An understanding of internal controls and procedures for financial reporting
- An understanding of audit committee functions

The audit committee financial expert must have acquired these qualifications through experience as a principal financial officer, accounting officer, public accountant, controller, or auditor; or experience actively supervising one of these; or experience overseeing or assessing the performance of companies or public accountants in the preparation, auditing, or evaluation of financial statements.

The standards for a director to qualify as a financial expert are high, and they should be. While the fundamentals of key financial statements (profit and loss, balance sheet, cash flow) are simple, in large companies these statements can be extraordinarily complex with apparently precise numbers masking myriad estimates, judgments, and other less-than-precise determinations.

Financial literacy requirements are not as stringent as those for the financial expert. They include the ability to read and analyze (in a basic way) financial statements and accompanying notes and to understand accounting policies, estimates, and judgments. Still, I believe that every director (not just those on the audit committee) should have the ability and determination to forge through many pages of financial statements, footnotes, and management discussion and analysis to exercise proper fiduciary diligence and, on behalf of shareholders, know the company's true financial condition.

It's great if a person has the requisite financial literacy or expertise to be a director. If not, it's essential to acquire it. Nothing undermines a director's credibility and gravitas in *all* domains like weakness with the numbers.

As a motivator for the education that may be needed, let me share a few insights from my son, Brian, who is a faculty member in accounting at the University of Texas at Austin. At my request, he made a presentation on analysis of financial statements to an undergraduate class I teach composed mainly of nonbusiness majors. He concluded with some points that rang true to me as a long-time director and on which I think any financially literate director should be able to write an informed essay:

- Financial statements use a standardized format and measurement to facilitate comparisons

- Accrual-based accounting can make accounting information more useful to reflect underlying economics

- Accruals require judgment and discretion—there is a tradeoff between better information and potential for abuse

- Financial statement numbers are only useful in context and with some transformation including vertical/horizontal income statements and ratio analysis.

If a director is not ready to write these essays, financial literacy education is in order. Consider a *finance for non-financial managers* executive education course or a *financial statements analysis* course at a local business school.

A Human Community

One day when I was working at Cummins, word arrived that the mother of one of our colleagues on the president's staff had died, the victim of a hit-and-run driver. The funeral was several days later, in a town hundreds of miles away from our headquarters in Columbus, Indiana, and it conflicted with an important meeting. Of course we extended our condolences. But, in addition, Jim Henderson, the president, said that he would be going to the funeral and invited those of us who wished to attend. I did. It was a sad experience, but it felt good to provide in-person support to our colleague and his family.

There was some quiet contention among the staff about the wisdom of Jim's decision to take the time to attend the funeral in light of the difficult business conditions we were facing and the meeting that was displaced. I spoke about this with Irwin Miller, Cummins' founding father. I'll never forget what Irwin said: "*The company is a family, and we put family things first—always.*" I realized at that moment that Jim Henderson was president of Cummins in part because it was normal and natural for him, and much in line with Irwin's philosophy, to put a family matter first when it arose.

Irwin's view of the company as family was an exceptionally strong version of the idea that a company is a human community. Perhaps it doesn't have currency in much of corporate America today. Lest you dismiss it too quickly, though, let me note that Irwin's assertion was not the first time I'd encountered the idea of company as family. I heard the concept from a great teacher I had at the Harvard Business School, Dr. Harry Levinson. Harry was a rare thing: a psychoanalytically trained psychologist teaching in a business school. Harry taught us that a lot of behavior in companies is best understood by the simple fact that in important ways, organizational structure replicates family structure.

Trouble with the boss? Unresolved conflict with parents. Can't get along with coworkers? Sibling rivalry. Denial of obvious reality? Psychological defense. Bottomless need for approval? Maybe Mom and Dad didn't do their parenting jobs well, or maybe you didn't do your job of growing up.

Are these valid explanations? I don't know; I'm not a psychologist. But I was a leader in large organizations for a long time and I observed that the family metaphor for organizational life has merit. Habits of mind and heart developed in the home certainly play out in the workplace.

I continue today to see the leaders of some companies—especially private, family-owned companies—treat employees as an extension of their own families. This is the case at Gordon Food Service.

And employees reciprocate. When Paul Gordon became ill and died several years ago at the age of eighty-five, there was an outpouring of support and affection that had the unmistakable feeling of love for the great father of a very large family.

Why should directors remember that companies are human communities, even families?

First, when the board appoints a CEO, it also appoints the leader of the community and head of the family. Yes, he or she is the senior executive of an economic enterprise and will be judged on financial results. But day-to-day, the leader also needs to tend the community. That means participating in rituals and ceremonies, celebrating and grieving, and recognizing and supporting people.

Second, directors must be attuned to actions or policies that will affect the community—positively or negatively. In the first session of my undergraduate class, I assign a case study on Burt's Bees, a health and beauty aids company that emphasizes natural ingredients. The CEO at the time of the case initiates an aggressive program to reduce waste (the amount of stuff that ends up in a landfill) at Burt's Bees. This is obviously smart business because waste is cost. But the students also note how engaged Burt's Bees's employees are in the initiative. They're proud as a community that the company is being environmentally responsible because this is a value most members share. By contrast, I recall how upset people at Kraft (food) were when Philip Morris (tobacco) acquired the company in 1988. I knew Kraft employees who felt it was a violation of their values to be affiliated with the tobacco industry. Financial considerations drove the deal, of course, and today, after a variety of acquisitions and mergers, Kraft is unrelated to the tobacco business.

A third reason directors should recognize the community nature of a company is that doing so can strengthen bonds between employees and the company and save the shareholders money. If a company is seen only through an economic lens, then incentives are all about money. But employees, including executives, are human. Chris Argyris, a Yale professor, helped popularize the term *psychological contract* to describe important dimensions of the relationship between a company and its employees. The psychological contract includes mutual commitments and expectations, some of which are non-economic, such as being part of a company in which you can take pride; being treated fairly; having opportunities to learn, grow and develop; and having your achievements recognized. These are powerful things with people, yet most of them cost little or nothing.

To illustrate, I've had a lifelong affection for Cummins even though I only worked there for six years. As I was finishing my MBA, I interviewed with the company despite being close to deciding to continue my education in a PhD program. The interview went well. I told Ted Marson, the vice president for personnel, that I really liked Cummins but thought I wanted to be a professor and so was considering doing a PhD. I subsequently received an offer to join the company. I was torn. A few days later, Ted called and said something extraordinary: "Joe, we'd love to have you join Cummins. But I think faculty work is your calling. So do the PhD. Cummins will be around, and this won't be our last encounter."

I couldn't believe that the representative of a big company whose job was recruiting would put my interest first.

Ted turned out to be right on all counts. Faculty work was my calling. The PhD was the right path, and Cummins turned out to be part of my life for a long time: as a site for my dissertation research, as a consulting and executive education client, and ultimately as my employer for six eventful years where, for a while, Ted was my boss. More than thirty years after leaving Cummins' employment, I still feel loyal and bonded to the company!

A Story

Headhunters (executive recruiters) use the term *helicopter view* to describe a particular intellectual perspective that some people seem to possess more than others. It means the inclination or ability to rise above the immediate situation and look behind, ahead, and sideways in order to see connections, patterns, and themes.

It is important for directors to develop a helicopter view of the company they govern. A convenient gateway is simply to ask the question, "What is this company's story?" Every company has one.

There are multiple chapters featuring stages of development, notable people, achievements, and crises. These chapters have a powerful influence on the company's outlook, beliefs, value system, and character. To position the company for the future, it is exceedingly useful for directors to understand and honor the past.

Every organization has triumphant and traumatic episodes in its past that affect today's thinking—the equivalent of preferences and scar tissue in an individual's personality. For example, shortly after I became a director of GFS, I noticed that in discussions of food manufacturers, Kraft was seldom mentioned and, when it was, the tone was a little grim. This was despite the fact that Kraft was and is an important supplier to GFS. I inquired as to why and learned that earlier in the company's history, Kraft had withdrawn Gordon's franchise to sell Kraft products in western Michigan and nearly put the company—and the current generation's great-grandfather—out of business. How much earlier did this occur? Five decades! But traumatic memories linger in companies as in individuals.

So do triumphant memories, sometimes to great advantage. Consider, for example, the story of how GFS went from being a U.S.-only business in 1990 to a prominent, coast-to-coast food service distributor in Canada today.

GFS is a growth company. Until the early 1990s, that growth was achieved organically—that is, without acquisitions. But when companies become large, they often need and have the resources to grow through acquisitions in addition to organic growth. So in the mid-nineties, GFS acquired the Ontario and Quebec food service subsidiary of a large Canadian food company. We were all excited about our first significant acquisition and about becoming international. That was until the acquisition persisted in losing money at an increasing rate.

We tried a lot of things. Nothing worked until we found a couple of Canadian entrepreneurial owners who joined forces with GFS Canada, turned things around to their benefit and ours, and grew profitable food service operations in Toronto and Quebec. For us, the lesson was indelible. We didn't want to buy the operations of large companies and adopt their managers. We wanted people like the Gordons: scrappy entrepreneurs who had built their businesses from the ground up, knew how to treat their customers and employees well, and were determined to grow while being tough about capital expenditures and operating expenses. Once we'd learned these lessons and knew what we wanted, GFS acted fast. We made a series of acquisitions that fit this profile and in just a few short years created a large, successful, coast-to-coast business in Canada.

Every company's story has chapters. Yesterday's chapters can inform the writing of tomorrow's by the board and senior management. Here's one more example.

I joined Cummins in 1981. Cummins had a good run in the 1970s as oil prices rose and fuel economy became a priority for truckers and heavy equipment operators. Inflation was high, but Cummins was proficient at raising prices and making them stick.

That is, until Ronald Reagan became president in 1981 and he and Paul Volcker, chairman of the Federal Reserve System, determined to slay the inflation dragon through tight monetary policy and sky-high interest rates. The result was a wicked recession that cut deeply into Cummins' business and precipitated the most difficult conditions for us since the Great Depression. The survival of a proud company, founded in 1919, was at stake. We had to cut costs, deep and fast.

Adding to the misery, we began to see foreign competitors arrive on U.S. shores from both Europe (e.g., Daimler) and Japan (e.g., Hino and Komatsu) with good products and prices lower than ours.

Cummins' chairman, Henry Schacht, and president, Jim Henderson, put their heads together and, with the support of the board, forged a strategy for Cummins' short-term survival and long-term success. It was daunting, easier to conceptualize than implement. All we had to do, Henry and Jim told us, was cut prices and costs 30 percent in 30 months while spending millions to develop an entirely new 10-liter engine to replace our bread-and-butter 14-liter product and invest in a new plant in which to build it!

What led Schacht and Henderson to formulate such an audacious strategy? Two things, in my view: indelible lessons from an early chapter in Cummins' history and a very painful chapter in the modern history of the U.S. auto industry.

Cummins' history was unique. Clessie Lyle Cummins was the driver, mechanic, and handyman for the Irwin family that was prominent in Columbus, Indiana, early in the twentieth century. Clessie was fascinated by the diesel engine and, with the support of the family, founded Cummins as an engine company in 1919, about twenty-five years after Rudolf Diesel's development of the engine that bears his name. Cummins did not turn a profit until 1937; the family funded *eighteen years* of losses. Profitability was the result of Cummins launching the Model H engine in 1933 into the teeth of the Great Depression.

For us, the lessons of this early chapter were indelible: be tough, be patient, invest in the future, focus on quality, and take the long view. So in 1981, in the face of a brutal recession and daunting strategic challenges, it was our turn to put to work these lessons from Cummins' early history. We found them reassuring. It's not like we hadn't been here before. They helped us succeed.

Lessons from a then-recent chapter in the history of the Big Three auto companies—General Motors, Ford, and Chrysler—increased our resolve and sense of urgency to implement our strategy. We had watched these three companies go from literally owning the U.S. automotive market in the 1950s and '60s to suffering steady inroads from foreign manufacturers, at first European (e.g., the VW Beetle) and later, Japanese (Honda and Toyota). The result was a slow but dramatic loss of market share over several decades. We studied this history and came to three conclusions:

- The Big Three had raised a price umbrella that made it attractive for foreign manufacturers to enter the U.S. market and, with their lower costs, undercut domestic manufacturers in price while earning enough to fund new product development and expansion.

- Better quality, at least as much as lower prices, was attracting American buyers from the Big Three to foreign competitors who were proving that better quality did not have to mean higher costs and prices.

- Once consumers chose products from foreign manufacturers and were satisfied, it was almost impossible to win them back, implying a permanent loss of market share for the Big Three.

With these lessons in mind, we deemed our strategy of drastically reducing costs and prices while developing new products and improving quality to be essential, not optional.

Did it work? The big picture answer is certainly yes. Cummins has not only survived but thrived over the last thirty years and in 2013 had revenues of over $17 billion and a market capitalization of $25 billion. In the relay race of leadership, CEOs appointed by the Cummins board over the last 40 years—Henry Schacht, Jim Henderson, Tim Solso, and now Tom Linebarger—have enabled Cummins to survive and thrive. Tim Solso did a superb job as CEO between 2000 and 2012. He was appointed chairman of the board of General Motors in 2013. His views on governance are included in interviews with directors on which I report in Chapter 7.

I hope it's evident how important and valuable it is for directors of a company to understand the company's story and how it can influence decisions to create a stronger, better tomorrow.

A Means and an End

A successful company can enable its owners and others to build something of inherent value and achieve goals important to them. Here's a vivid illustration.

I first met Tom Monaghan in 1975 when I was a newly minted assistant professor at the University of Michigan Business School. I was trying to recruit companies for my students to examine as live case studies. It was difficult. I was young, my students were young, and a lot of doors were slammed in my face.

I was aware of a small, private company headquartered in Ann Arbor called Domino's Pizza. I decided to approach the CEO on the theory that my students were his customers and this might improve the odds of our gaining access. I made an appointment and arrived at Domino's headquarters in a corrugated steel building on I-94. An assistant showed me into an unpretentious office and there, seated in a chair behind a large desk, was the founder, owner, and CEO of Domino's, Tom Monaghan. What caught my attention was the art on the wall behind him: a gorgeous, top-down, color photograph of a pizza. This was my introduction to business owners' love of their product.

Tom was (and is) an interesting man with a compelling personal story. His father died when he was four, and his mother, struggling, gave Tom and his brother to a Catholic orphanage where he was raised from ages six to twelve. Taught by nuns, he came to love his Catholic faith. Like many kids in Michigan, he also loved the Detroit Tigers. He yearned for a better life and, surely, security.

Though Tom enrolled at the University of Michigan with the goal of becoming an architect, work and business intervened in the form of a small pizza store in Ypsilanti, Michigan, adjacent to Ann Arbor, called DomiNick's. Tom and his brother borrowed $500 and purchased it. After opening three more stores, Tom gave his brother a Volkswagen Beetle in exchange for his half of the business. The rest, as they say, is history. Tom pioneered pizza delivery and focused on communities with college campuses or military bases—densely housed, hungry young people with few cars. Through franchising, the company grew like wildfire. In 1998, Tom sold Domino's to Bain Capital for an estimated $1 billion.

During the years I lived in Ann Arbor, I noted that Domino's provided Tom with respect, security, and a good life. The company had inherent value: it was a source of challenge, achievement, and pride for Tom as well as employment and wealth creation for thousands of franchisees, employees, and suppliers. It also poignantly enabled Tom to fulfill big dreams:

- He acquired and owned the Detroit Tigers from 1983 to 1992.

- He built a Frank Lloyd Wright–inspired, prairie-style corporate headquarters in Ann Arbor and became a foremost collector of Wright artifacts.

- He collected classic automobiles, including one of the world's six Bugatti Royales.

- He purchased an island off Michigan's Upper Peninsula where he generously hosted friends.

These were fairly normal dreams for a wealthy man. What was even more interesting to me was Tom's decision in the early 1990s to divest himself of most of his worldly possessions, including the Detroit Tigers and the huge, half-finished Wright-inspired mansion that was to be his home, and devote his wealth almost exclusively to his Catholic faith. His works have included building a cathedral in Managua, Nicaragua, to replace one destroyed in a 1972 earthquake; creating the Ave Maria Foundation; founding a Catholic college and law school named Ave Maria; commissioning the *Ave Maria Mass* by composer Stephen Edwards; and transforming the college into Ave Maria University and building a home for it in a new town he established, Ave Maria, Florida, in Collier County, thirty miles east of Naples.

See what I mean about a company being a means as well as an end? Domino's Pizza, a company with a prosaic product and humble beginnings, made all this possible for Tom Monaghan.

Companies are important to more than just their owners. Let me draw a parallel to another kind of institution that I know well: a nonprofit.

I have spent my career at two great public universities. I think the best book ever written on such institutions is *Uses of the University* by Clark Kerr, long-time president of the University of California.[17] A major theme is that a wide variety of individuals and groups feel they own and have the right to influence and use public universities to achieve their goals. I can report from first-hand experience that this is true. When I was president of the University of Illinois, I was struck by the passion that students, faculty, staff, alumni, elected officials, and citizens of Illinois brought to issues that arose. On my watch, these included the missions of the university, the ratio of resident to non-resident students, admissions practices, online education, and sustainability. Believe me, I never said to any of hundreds of thousands of U of I stakeholders, "I'm sorry, the university doesn't belong to you, your view doesn't matter!"

The sense of ownership of companies is not nearly as broad as with a public university because companies have well-defined and legally established owners. Still, a wise corporate board understands that many parties have a strong sense of *psychological* ownership of a company even if they have no legal ownership whatsoever. This is because a company can be a powerful means to achieving goals or ends they care about.

When I was dean of the business school at Michigan, I partnered with the dean of the school of natural resources and environment to create an interesting and, at the time, controversial joint program between our schools. Fred Erb, a Michigan graduate, and his wife, Barbara, believed in our concept and funded the creation of what is now called the Erb Institute for Global Sustainable Enterprise. We knew there were students who wanted education in both business and natural resources and the environment so they could join companies and nonprofits and help guide them toward more sustainable practices. They saw companies as not just the cause of but also the solution to environmental problems. They appreciated the mission of nonprofits but knew they need to be run in a business-like way to be successful. The program built on initiatives like the McDonald's Corporation / Environmental Defense Fund partnership that began in 1990 to phase out polystyrene clamshell food containers. The partnership has endured for over 20 years and, according to the EDF website, eliminated 300 million pounds of packaging, recycled a million tons of corrugated boxes, and reduced waste by 30 percent in its first decade.

People can also have strong feelings about a company because of practices with which they *disagree*. One of my favorite cases to teach involves Nike Corporation and opposition to some of its labor practices (sweatshops) abroad.[18] Narrowly speaking, if Nike's board is striving to maximize long-run shareholder value and obeying the laws of the lands where it operates, what business is it of non-owners to question what goes on inside Nike plants? The answer, of course, is that people who care make it their business. The case describes the means and methods used by advocates to persuade Nike to change its practices in line with their views and values.

Directors should recognize that the companies they oversee have inherent value—that is, they are ends in themselves. In addition, they can also serve as powerful means for people to achieve goals they value.

An Open System

A few books and teachers affect the way we see things the rest of our lives. That was the case for me with a book on organizations as open systems by Daniel Katz and Robert L. Kahn, *The Social Psychology of Organizations*, and my subsequent interactions with Bob Kahn, one of the finest teachers I've known.[19]

Prior to Katz and Kahn, books on organizations, including management tomes and sociological and psychological treatments of the subject, had an intensely internal focus, as if organizations existed in splendid isolation. Katz and Kahn borrowed open system theory from biology and applied its key concepts to organizations. They recognized that organizations, as social phenomena, share basic characteristics with cells as biological phenomena. The core dynamic is *exchange* between the entity and its environment. System characteristics include input-throughput-output, negative entropy (the need to combat the natural tendency of systems to wind down over time), system boundaries, and interdependence with the environment.

Most people see organizations as pyramids of authority or networks. I see them this way also. But ever since reading Katz and Kahn, I have viewed organizations as living organisms engaged in exchange relationships with their environments, offering things of value, receiving resources in return, and using those resources to secure new inputs. I am attuned to problems that can develop in the exchange relationship and, if not remedied, cause serious disability or death. I am aware that if boundaries are too rigid, exchange is difficult and entropy sets in; if they are too permeable, disorder and chaos can result.

Are these helpful views for a director? Probably not for everybody, but they are for me. For example, as chair of the governance committee at EQR, I have been delighted to help recruit new, younger directors who have an experience-based understanding of our residents, who tend to be young. I think of it as one way to increase the permeability of the boundaries of the company with our environment. And I remember engaging in spirited discussions with Paul and John Gordon and Dave Gray twenty-five years ago about what would be required to keep GFS a growing, dynamic company, successfully combating entropy, as the entrepreneurial founders receded from active service. Some of the ideas we had, like having a strong CEO to avoid management by committee, requiring stretch annual and five-year performance goals, and providing financial incentives for high performance, seem to have worked.

Why Board Diversity Matters

I believe that a board is better, stronger, and richer as a result of the different takes on the company of directors with different experiences, expertise, and habits of mind. To me, this is the most important meaning of and reason for diversity on a board. Yes, diversity of age, race, and gender are valuable, especially in terms of expanding the talent pool and connecting with the broad groups that make up our society. But a board can have exemplary diversity along these dimensions and miss the deeper kind of diversity I am pointing out.

Several years ago at EQR, we experienced a number of normal departures from our board. As a result, we needed to recruit new directors. We spent considerable time defining what we were seeking through the search process. In one such conversation, Sam Zell cut to the chase with the following observation:

> Look, all the things you say we want are important. But when the dust settles, let's make sure that we have on our board some people whose ages begin with four or five instead of six or seven and who understand the world the way our residents do.

As a result, we added to our board four outstanding people: two men and two women, younger than the then-current directors and much in tune with social media, networking, entrepreneurship, and other things we know are important to EQR residents. Mary Kay Haben has held senior positions at Kraft Foods and Wrigley and also serves on the boards of Bob Evans and Hershey. Brad Keywell is a serial entrepreneur and cofounder of Groupon. Mark Shapiro has had executive experience at ESPN, Six Flags, Dick Clark Productions, and Live Nation. Linda Walker-Bynoe is an accomplished African-American director of multiple companies including Northern Trust and Prudential Retail Mutual Funds.

A traditional approach to board recruiting in this case would have focused on candidates with years of experience in multi-family real estate. We value people with these abilities, of course, and expect every trustee to learn the business. But we have three board members who have spent their careers in the industry and others whose experience is adjacent to it. In addition, years of experience can quickly translate into restricting a search to candidates who reinforce the "pale, male, and stale" profile of many boards.

It goes without saying that our new trustees' take on a company is somewhat different than mine based on an academic career and large company executive and director experience. And it's different than other independent EQR trustees with backgrounds in real estate, banking, and finance. The diversity is good—exactly what we wanted. Under new disclosure requirements, we state in EQR's annual proxy exactly why we believe each trustee is qualified to serve and how each adds value.

Nonprofit Governance— How and Why It's Different

There are more than 1.5 million nonprofit organizations registered in the United States. They include public charities, private foundations, schools, churches, hospitals, chambers of commerce, fraternal organizations, and civic leagues. Many have boards of directors.

I have served on and reported to nonprofit boards. There are similarities to corporate boards but also some important differences:

- Nonprofit boards are usually larger. Because nonprofits use their boards to build loyalty and raise money, some have twenty-five, fifty, or even more directors. An executive committee of the board often performs key governance functions.

- Directors are not paid. In fact, they are usually expected to contribute. It's wise to ask what the financial expectations are before agreeing to join a nonprofit board.

- The board's governance responsibilities are often shared with others. In many nonprofits, *shared governance* is a reality. In hospitals, it is with the physicians. In universities, it is with the faculty.

- A nonprofit CEO's authority is seldom as strong as a corporate CEO's as a result of shared governance, fewer financial incentives, and a more benign environment when it comes to accountability.

- The objective function of the organization—what it is trying to maximize or optimize—is not as clear as in the corporate world where profit and loss and market value send powerful signals.

Despite these differences, in my experience the most important aspects of board work are identical in the nonprofit and for-profit worlds. Directors are stewards. The Pyramid of Purpose applies. The board must understand the organization in all of the dimensions discussed in this chapter.

Nonprofit board work can be extremely gratifying because of directors' strong identification with the mission of the organization —education, health care, faith, community, and so on. I was extremely grateful to members of the several boards (Visiting Committee, Alumni, Development) that worked closely with me to build the quality, stature, and funding of the University of Michigan Business School during the decade I served as dean. We couldn't have done it without them. I also appreciated their patience because nonprofit organizations tend to move at a more measured (to put it politely) pace than their corporate counterparts. This can be hard on directors from the corporate world!

Conclusion

Every organization means many things to many people. Directors need to understand them all in order to serve as capable stewards.

We turn next to the substance of the board's work. Good stewardship—great governance—requires that directors do the right things.

CHAPTER 4

Do the Right Things

The Substance of Great Governance

Earlier I asked the question, "What is great governance?" In this chapter and the next, I answer the question in detail.

Experience and research point to a top-ten list of things a board must do for management and the organization to thrive:

1. Set high performance aspirations and a proper tone at the top
2. Appoint an excellent leader and plan for succession
3. Help develop and approve a winning strategy
4. Approve annual and long range plans and monitor results
5. Create incentives for desired performance
6. Ensure quality financial reporting and effective internal controls
7. Oversee a balance sheet with ample liquidity and prudent debt
8. Oversee enterprise risk
9. Be vigilant about capital investments, especially acquisitions

10. Assist management in uniquely useful ways

There is one additional thing that directors must do for themselves:

• Renew the board

These items compose a board's vital checklist of the right things to do.

Set High Performance Aspirations and a Proper Tone at the Top

High Aspirations

In Chapter 1, I discussed the importance of high aspirations for an organization. I quoted the late CEO of Motorola, Bob Galvin, who said that the very least leadership can do is to set high aspirations because they are antecedent to high performance.

I took this advice to heart when I was dean at Michigan. I sensed that our students and faculty had a chronic, mild inferiority complex relative to other top B-schools like Harvard, Stanford, Wharton, and Kellogg. I proposed to the business school's Visiting Committee, our most senior board, that we publicly articulate this goal: to be the world's best business school and be recognized as such. I don't know that we ever fully achieved that goal, but under this banner, we became the leader in combining classroom education with real world professional development, were rated as the nation's most innovative business school, improved our rankings and, in one memorable year, had the number one undergraduate business program and number two MBA program in America. I heard "Michigan" a lot more in hallway conversation among members of our community and fewer mentions of our competitors. And it wasn't just the immediate community members who believed. In the decade I was dean, our alumni and friends contributed over $100 million to the school and helped grow our endowment from $30 million to over $250 million. High aspirations paid off.

Many boards and CEOs have learned that a simple means of developing and communicating high aspirations is a mission or vision statement. For example, here is Gordon Food Service's mission statement:

> Our purpose is to serve our customers with the highest-quality foodservice products and services. We achieve this purpose through innovative systems and the spirit and integrity of our people.

Mission and vision statements help set a high aspiration level. When brought alive in new employee orientation, ongoing education and training, and leadership actions consistent with the statements, they become an integral part of the organization's culture. It is valuable to tell stories from the company's history that illustrate people's dedication to the mission. A staple at GFS are stories of sales people making heroic efforts to secure an essential food product and personally deliver it to a restaurant customer so the show can go on.

In addition to high aspirations, the board must establish the proper tone at the top.

Tone at the Top

I first encountered this term while participating as a young faculty member in a major study of internal control[20] sponsored by the Financial Executives Research Foundation (FERF) of the Financial Executives Institute (now Financial Executives International). The study was headed by Bob Mautz, a legendary professor of accounting at the University of Illinois, a partner at Ernst & Ernst, and director of the Paton Accounting Center at the University of Michigan, where I met him. In the aftermath of international corporate bribery scandals by U.S. companies and the passage of the Foreign Corrupt Practices Act by Congress in 1977, FERF asked Bob to lead a field-based examination of internal control in U.S. companies. He assembled an interdisciplinary team of young faculty members from accounting, finance, information technology, and organizational behavior, which was my field.

We did a literature review then visited over a hundred companies across the United States, where we interviewed CEOs, CFOs, and other members of management. A funny thing happened on the way to our conclusions. We found that while policies, procedures, and systems were all important in ensuring good internal control and avoiding fraud and corruption, other things were more important. They included the environment created and expectations communicated by senior management through their words and example. The soft outweighed the hard when it came to good internal control. We called these soft elements the *tone at the top* of the organization. While I doubt we invented the term, our study helped popularize it.

Tone at the top gained even greater currency following accounting scandals that occurred around 2000 and brought down entire companies, including Enron, Tyco, Adelphia, and WorldCom. Postmortems suggested that the tone at the top had permitted, if not encouraged, practices that undermined effective internal control and quality financial reporting. The term was emphasized in the Sarbanes-Oxley Act of 2002, the legislative response to these scandals.

Today, *tone at the top* has graduated from the accounting function to a concept signifying the organization-wide ethical climate. Responsibility for the proper tone at the top lies squarely with the board and senior management.

In my experience, boards set the tone at the top through the people they appoint, the words that they and those they appoint say, and the actions they take.

Here's an example of the power of action in setting a tone. Cummins' president, Jim Henderson, gave many speeches on quality when I worked with him. Today, I can't remember just what he said. But I remember like it was yesterday his shutting down the Jamestown Assembly Plant engine line until the cause of an unexplained oil consumption problem was found and fixed. Jim took this action despite our distributors and OEM customers demanding delivery of more of the new engines being built there. The problem was found and fixed. One courageous action to protect quality was worth thousands of words when it came to setting a tone in the company. People need to see you mean what you say.

It's important for the board to appoint leaders who *walk the talk* and back them when they do. Boards also need to walk the talk themselves. As with parents and their children, leaders' actions speak louder than words as a means of conveying important values.

Appoint an Excellent Leader and Plan for Succession

A board's most important responsibility is to appoint the organization's chief executive officer. This decision, more than any other, will affect the success of the enterprise and reflect on the judgment of the board.

When the board gets the CEO appointment right, being a director is a pleasure. Things will go as well as they possibly can, no matter how difficult the environment or challenging the problems. When it's wrong, there is hell to pay. Performance will suffer. Policy differences will emerge between the CEO and the board. Directors will likely divide over those who support the CEO and think he or she deserves more time and those who believe new leadership is essential, the sooner the better. By the time the dust settles and the board agrees to make a change, costly months or years will have passed. Fingers crossed, the board will try all over again to find the right leader.

What does it mean to get it right when it comes to appointing a CEO? The new leader must

- *be right for the situation*, that is, have the smarts to develop a good game plan and the skills to execute it successfully;
- *be accepted by the organization* so authority conferred by the board translates into effective leadership; and
- *stay long enough* to achieve critical goals and set the stage for smooth succession.

I watched with pleasure the appointment of my classmate, Tim Solso, as Cummins' CEO in 2000 and his and Cummins' hard-won success in the ensuing decade. Tim was a great appointment by the Cummins board. He met all three of the criteria for a new CEO.

Cummins went from struggling for survival to thriving during his twelve years of service. Sales doubled, and the share price soared from a low of $4.28 in 2002 to well over $100. Tim's and his team's performance made the Cummins board look very, very good.

I, too, have had the pleasure of participating in the appointment of CEOs who made directors look smart. Gordon Food Service prospered with the leadership of Dan Gordon and continues to do so with his brother, Jim, as CEO. The same is true of David Neithercut at EQR. I knew David twenty years ago when he was a bright, young CFO. It has been a pleasure to see him develop into an extraordinarily able CEO, operating at the top of his game.

A challenge in appointing the right CEO is that directors carry in their minds different images of what will constitute a successful leader. Realizing this, I set out several years ago to explore my own thinking on the subject and share it with others. The result was a book, *The Nature of Leadership*.[21] In it, I present a simple framework for thinking about the dimensions that a board should take into account when considering CEOs and other candidates for senior leadership. I call it the Leadership Pyramid:

Leadership Pyramid

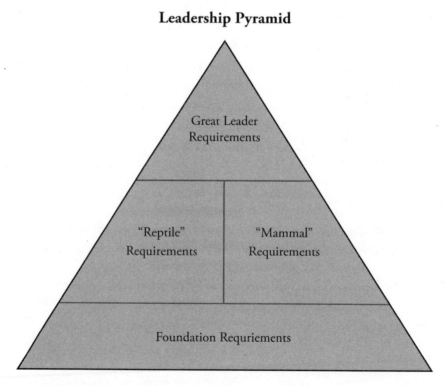

Start with the foundation requirements at the base of the Pyramid. Leadership is hard, and you really have to want the job. Many of us wonder why anyone would endure the rigors, nonsense, and character assassination of a run for the U.S. presidency. Yet there are always plenty of candidates. Why? Ego plays a role, but the best motive is a desire to serve others. In addition, because senior leadership is a marathon, you need the ability, strength, and character to run it successfully. Of these, character is most important. Shortcomings in abilities and strength can be supplemented with other people, but character can't be delegated.

In the center of the Pyramid are the hard and soft sides of leadership. For fun, in my book I refer to them as *reptile* and *mammal* characteristics, drawing on an annual summer faculty softball game at the University of Michigan Business School between the Reptiles (economics-trained faculty) and Mammals (behavioral science–trained faculty). While leaders tend more toward one or the other of these types, the best leaders have the ability to be both *warm as toast* and *tough as nails*.

At the top of the Pyramid is pay dirt: a leader's ability to *make change*. Organizations must respond to never-ending changes in their environments, technology, competition, and customers. Adaptation is essential. Sometimes the change is wrenching. When at Cummins we had to reduce our costs to support reducing our prices by as much as 30 percent during a 30-month sprint, the change was fast and hard. Sometimes the pace can be more benign, but not often.

Leading change while producing excellent results is the ultimate test of every CEO. Directors need assurance that the leader they appoint will pass the test. The stakes, sometimes including the survival of the organization, couldn't be higher.

It's not enough for a board to appoint an excellent leader. The process leading to the appointment is also important. Most of the time, CEO succession should be planned, orderly, and as dramatic as watching paint dry. Signs of failure include a dearth of internal candidates, a destructively competitive horse race, or an outside search by a board with its back to the wall. Contrary to the impression created by press coverage of CEO succession, most of the time the process is not newsworthy. Rather, it is the result of developing internal candidates over many years so that when the time comes, the successor is obvious or the board has several well-qualified candidates from which to choose.

I mentioned earlier Tim Solso's appointment and great decade-long run as CEO of Cummins. Tim already had *thirty years* at Cummins under his belt when he became CEO. Check out the career histories of the CEOs of rock-solid American companies such as Caterpillar, Procter & Gamble, and UPS. It's the same pattern: a smooth succession of strong internal candidates who accept the baton in the relay race of leadership, then provide the requisite mixture of stability and change to maintain the strength of these iconic companies.

There are times when such succession is not possible. Bill Ford found himself in this situation at Ford Motor Company in the mid-2000s and, greatly to his and the board's credit, recognized that the beleaguered company desperately needed an injection of talent from outside the company and auto industry. Alan Mulally from Boeing turned out to be a savior. Ford survived the Great Recession without bankruptcy or a government bailout and has prospered since.[22] Sometimes a CEO dies or departs before successor candidates are ready for the job. Sometimes a good housecleaning is needed and the right broom is an outside hire. In these cases, directors need to be like a good jazz quartet: adept at improvisation. Still, boards should strive for smooth, effective internal succession.

Help Develop, then Approve, a Winning Strategy

Strategy is the way a company creates economic value or a nonprofit organization achieves its mission. Strategy is an organization's means of competing. It involves parlaying strengths and negating weaknesses in order to capitalize on opportunities and ward off threats. Strategy is an organization's means of surviving and thriving.

Strategy *formulation* takes place at the boundary of the board of directors and senior management. Strategy *execution* is solely the province of management. While many functions are well defined as either governance or management, the nature of strategy formulation makes it both. A good board knows it cannot impose strategy on management because execution requires conviction. And wise management does not simply take strategy to the board for endorsement. Ideally, the board and management, led by the latter, work together to think through, develop, understand, and *own* strategy.

There are two reasons. First, strategy is so important that every senior person, whether in governance or management, should be in the process of helping figure it out, challenging it, and making sure it's right. Second, strategy execution in the business and nonprofit worlds, as in war, always entails setbacks and failures. Finger pointing between the board and management at such times is not helpful. Far better is an attitude that *we* committed to this path, *we* are encountering problems, *we* either need to persist or modify, and *we* are committed to succeeding with the present strategy or agreeing on a new one. .

I don't mean to sound naïve here. The board and management are in a hierarchical relationship, and if there is a pattern of poor results over a sustained period, it will be incumbent on the board to oust management and put in place people who can succeed. But that is very different than an unconvinced management trying to execute board-imposed strategy or a board cutting and running when management's recommended strategy turns out to be more arduous than anticipated. Here's an example.

In my inaugural address as president of the University of Illinois in 2005, I offered as an illustration of innovative thinking the following statement: "What if we could combine the academic quality of the University of Illinois with the user-friendliness of the University of Phoenix?" This idea captured the imagination of the board of trustees as a means of generating new revenue and fulfilling our land-grant mission of extending quality education to thousands of people across Illinois and beyond who are place-bound and, therefore, unable to study at one of our campuses. Simultaneously, the idea alarmed some faculty, especially on the Urbana campus, which has a strong tradition of shared governance.

No matter how we addressed faculty concerns, they continued unabated. We tried at their suggestion to partner with the University's schools and colleges to create programs and courses. The pace was frustratingly slow. So we pursued separate accreditation for Global Campus. Faculty governance had a fit. This so frightened the board that they directed me to end the program even though we were in the launch stage and desperately working to achieve altitude. Money was wasted. Opponents of change were emboldened. Most regrettably, thousands of fully qualified, non-traditional students like single parents and working adults who could have benefited from a University of Illinois education were denied the opportunity.

As president, Global Campus's failure was my responsibility. I realize, in retrospect, that I'd involved the board only enough to excite them and earn their support to *launch* Global Campus but not enough to maintain their commitment through startup challenges that were inevitable. Lesson learned? Management must take the initiative on strategy, but the board and management together need to own the strategy for it to survive rough times and have a chance to succeed.

Strategy formulation is an intellectually demanding task. Some of the most valuable work to come out of top business schools and consulting firms is intended to help boards and senior management think about and develop strategy. I've had the privilege of personally knowing two of the top contributors. Michael Porter was a classmate who created the *five forces* model of corporate strategy, a groundbreaking piece of work that brought rigorous economic analysis to what had long been a common sense, case-oriented craft.[23] The late C. K. Prahalad was a faculty colleague and friend when I was dean at Michigan. C. K. was an original thinker. With his colleague, Gary Hamel, C. K. developed and popularized concepts and vocabulary like *strategic intent* and *core competence* that became mainstays in the minds and language of executives, consultants, and boards around the world. Late in his career, the Indian-born Prahalad challenged global corporations to stop ignoring the needs and aspirations of the world's poor. He asserted that the poor are just like the rest of us, with a desire for dignity, respect, opportunity, and improvement in their living standards. He argued that companies could grow their businesses and serve these customers profitably if only they understood them and incorporated serving them into their strategies.[24]

Strategy formulation and execution are intertwined with an organization's planning process. A long-range plan reflects and influences strategy. The annual operating plan is a critical means of executing strategy. The board must be sure these plans are in place, then monitor results against them.

Approve Annual and Long-range Plans and Monitor Results

With high aspirations, the proper tone at the top, an excellent leader in place, and strategy agreed, the board and management must settle into the vital routine of making plans, monitoring results, and adjusting as necessary. The best and simplest description I've encountered of this process originated in the quality movement. While I was at Cummins, we invited Professor Kaoru Ishikawa, Japan's great quality guru, to come to Columbus, Indiana, and teach us. One of his slides was simply a circle divided into four quadrants with the letters *PDCA* in them:

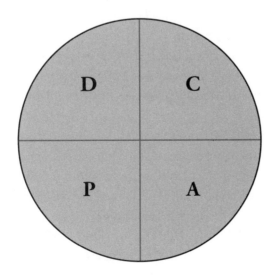

Professor Ishikawa explained that PDCA stands for *Plan, Do, Check, Act*, the never-ending cycle of continuous improvement of any process. For the board and senior management, the process is setting performance goals (Plan), achieving results (Do), understanding variances from plan (Check), and making adjustments based on analysis (Act). This process is the method by which the board and management together monitor and exercise control over the company's performance.

The board's most important *regularly recurring* work is approval of an annual operating plan (AOP) and long-range (typically five years) plan (LRP) that is updated annually, then monitoring results against the plans and, in the case of the AOP, the prior year's results.

There are many truisms about plans that can be helpful to directors. Jim Henderson, my boss at Cummins, used to say that in management, if you don't have a plan, you have nothing. My CPA father liked to say that a budget (the financial part of a plan) is a guide, not a straitjacket. W. Edwards Deming, an American quality guru, would remind managers that it's just as important to analyze and understand *positive* variances as negative because *all* variances signal a system not under control.

On every board, the most common question directors ask management is "How's business?" The most frequent answer is "We're on (or behind, or ahead of) plan." The answer tends to set a tone. *On plan* is reassuring, *behind plan* creates concern, and *ahead of plan* means breathing room.

Creation of the annual operating plan begins with two things: the prior year's results and what the LRP calls for in the coming year. To these inputs are added a projection of the coming year's business environment, likely pluses and minuses that will affect results, and management's judgment and gut feel. In general, both the board and senior management want to create a *stretch but achievable* plan. The board will usually be biased toward a little more stretch, the management toward achievable. This is healthy tension, motivated by the board's role representing shareholders who want to see higher earnings that will increase enterprise value, and management's desire to earn the maximum incentive pay that will be tied to results versus plan.

Development of the long-range plan is a far more creative task than the AOP. A key input is the plan's financial performance parameters. Based on industry benchmarks and owners' requirements, the LRP will need to show, for example, annual revenue growth of 8 percent, annual earnings growth of 15 percent, and unleveraged return on investment (ROI) of 12 percent. Other measures may be added such as return on assets (ROA) or cash flow (e.g., earnings before interest and taxes). Together, these measures create a standard for financial performance that drives creative thinking about products, services, pricing, and market strategies that can achieve target revenue growth; productivity and efficiency improvements and cost and expense management, which in combination with revenue can achieve needed profit margins and net profit results; and, investment in plant, equipment, and technology required to generate revenue at cost and expense levels called for in the plan while also keeping total investment at the level required to earn target returns.

Good plans seldom come together easily. In an annual operating plan, the line between stretch goals and fiction can be hard to discern. The line between achievable and sandbagging can also be fine. There is a lot of beneficial re-planning by management that takes place between the board's first review of a proposed AOP and its final approval of the plan. Senior management builds credibility with the board by working with its own team to push for the best possible performance—aggressive revenue growth and wringing out the fat—before requesting board approval.

In the long-range plan, truly consequential thinking can be triggered when the plan calls for achievement of certain financial performance targets and extrapolation of the current business indicates they won't be met over the five-year plan cycle. This gap analysis can lead to major change. If revenue growth is falling short, product and service innovation can be kicked up. Management may need to seriously consider non-organic growth through acquisitions and mergers. If costs are the problem, management will examine product redesign, supply chain streamlining, automation, outsourcing, and reduced staff levels. If returns are inadequate, product and customer profitability will be analyzed. The numerator of the return equation will be increased through revenue increases and cost reductions. The denominator will be reduced through elimination of non-productive investments and working capital investments harder. Here's an example of how consequential LRP-driven thinking and action can be.

Twenty years ago, the board of Gordon Food Service decided it was important for GFS to continue to be a high growth company. There are many advantages to growth, both financial and non-financial (e.g., it creates opportunities for employees and is a morale booster). GFS had achieved double-digit percentage revenue growth for most of its history. When we extrapolated our current business in the five-year plan, we saw that growth was going to slow because the company had become large (it's harder to be a high-growth large company than a high-growth small company) and the food service industry's growth rate was gradually slowing. So the board asked management to examine and report on what could be done to fill the growth gap (the difference between our desired and extrapolated growth rate in the LRP).

They did, and together we considered a wide variety of options: deepening penetration in current markets, more aggressive organic expansion beyond those markets, acquiring distributors, and even some food production possibilities. (I remember a chicken venture in Russia. It's fun to explore loony ideas in places you don't know—as long as you don't act on them.)

When the dust settled, we made two decisions that over time transformed the company. First, we decided to kick up the pace of opening new GFS Marketplace stores. These are retail stores that serve both foodservice (restaurants and institutions) and retail customers. At the time, we were on pace to have about 50 such stores by today; instead, as a result of the gap analysis, we have 150. Second, after rejecting the option of acquiring other U.S. distributors, usually because we didn't want to pay the high prices they were going for, we acquired a Canadian distributor with operations in Toronto and Quebec. Fast forward to today and we can see, in retrospect, that this was the first step in creating what is now GFS Canada, a large and successful coast-to-coast food service business in our neighbor to the north.

GFS Canada was the opposite of an instant success. The early years were really difficult. For a period of time, we lost money prodigiously, at least by our standards. Success came through a combination of persistence (I doubt a public company facing quarterly earnings pressures could have stayed the course), intensive efforts by the chairman, Dan Gordon, and our colleague Dave Gray finding the right people to run our business and pursuing, for over a decade, the vision of a national company. GFS Canada was a case study of board ownership of strategy contributing to persistence in making it successful. I read once that persistence is the most underestimated corporate strategy. That was certainly true here. I can also report that judgments about when to recognize failure and cut losses versus stay the course and double down on a strategy are among the most difficult a board must make.

To summarize, the board must ensure that management develops a long-range plan that can, with excellent performance, meet the financial goals set by the board in the context of the organization's strategy. Directors must also sign off on annual operating plans, ensuring they are stretch but achievable and contribute to measurable progress in execution of strategy. With these things done, the board faces a question: What can we do to help motivate the organization to achieve the goals imbedded in the plan? Most important is having leaders who are high achievers. Also important are incentives for success.

Create Incentives for Desired Performance

Incentives work. If there is one philosophical point on which business people agree, this is it.

There may be doubts and disputes about the matter elsewhere in society (e.g., should teachers earn merit pay based on student performance, or should health care professionals' pay be tied to patient outcomes?). But business people believe deeply in the power of incentives to drive performance. A maxim in business is that *what gets measured gets attention and what gets rewarded gets done.*

The board of directors, with the help of its compensation committee, converts this philosophical belief into plans and programs. The goal is *pay for performance.* A board needs to be able to say, "Yes, our CEO makes a lot of money. But it's been earned through value created for shareholders."

When people think about incentives and pay for performance in the corporate world, they almost always have an executive compensation frame of reference.

But in fact, incentives permeate the business world. In many excellent companies, nearly everybody is on some sort of incentive plan that relates their pay to how they perform. Naturally, lower paid people have less of their pay at risk because they can't afford a big shortfall in earnings. The total compensation of highly paid people can be 80 percent or more variable (i.e., the base salary they receive is a relatively small percentage of their total pay when they and the company perform well).

The board manages CEO compensation directly and, with the CEO, the compensation of the rest of senior management. If directors are wise, they also monitor compensation practices for the rest of the organization even though these are management's responsibility. There should be no surprises when it comes to comparing and contrasting executives' compensation with everyone else's. Critics may wonder if boards are even aware of the large gap between the pay of senior people and everyone else. They are, and as citizens, most care and have strong views about what is required to raise pay levels at the bottom and in the middle of the income pyramid. But as fiduciaries, directors' concern is competitive pay at every level to ensure the company has the talent needed to succeed.

Trends

How much and how to pay senior executives is a front-and-center board responsibility. It can be a complex topic, studded with multivariate models and plans written in legalese. But at the bottom, executive compensation is simple. Whereas most people have a salary or base wage (and perhaps a bonus opportunity) plus benefits, executives have five categories of compensation:

- Base salary
- Short-term incentive (annual bonus)
- Long-term incentive (stock, options, or something else)
- Perquisites (e.g., club memberships for business use)
- Benefits (e.g., health, retirement, life insurance)

In addition, some executives are beneficiaries of plans that compensate them in case of a change in control of the company or their job responsibilities. Sought-after CEOs sometimes have contracts that specify other conditions of employment.

Trends in these five elements of executive compensation are quite clear:

- Base salaries tend to be low relative to total compensation (though substantial by most people's standards).

- The variable or at risk portions of pay—short- and long-term incentives—are by far the largest part of the pay package and are tied to performance against the annual operating plan (short-term incentive) plus remaining on the job and, sometimes, achieving specified goals, such as return on assets or sales (long-term incentive).

- Granting restricted shares of stock has grown as the preferred form of equity compensation since an accounting rules change in 2004 that required stock options be expensed. The shares are restricted because there is usually a period of time over which the executive must remain employed before the shares vest (the executive takes ownership). The notion prior to 2004 that options were free was ridiculous and untrue, but many boards acted as if they were.

- Perquisites have shrunk dramatically in favor of executives spending their own money on things they care about.

- Benefits for executives tend to include the same package that other employees have plus, typically, a non-qualified (not covered by the federal ERISA law) retirement plan.

These changes have been spurred over the last twenty-five years by the shareholder value movement. Boards provide executives with a powerful financial incentive (the annual bonus) to achieve earnings increases that drive stock prices. They also grant company equity in the form of stock and options that align executives' financial interests with those of shareholders. As a result, the value of salaries and perquisites now pales in comparison with these pay-for-performance elements of compensation.

Controversy

Many observers applaud these changes. Nonetheless, executive compensation is always a controversial subject in American society. It's easy to understand why. CEOs of public companies make a lot of money. According to Equilar, the 200 highest paid public company executives in 2012 earned between a low of $11.1 million (Dan Akerson, chairman and CEO of General Motors) and a high of $96.2 million (Larry Ellison, chairman and CEO of Oracle).[25]

For some people, this is just too much money, and no amount of pointing to pay-for-performance and pay-at-risk is going to dissuade them. Groups like Occupy Wall Street and individuals like liberal economist and *New York Times* columnist Paul Krugman are outraged by the multiple between CEO and median worker compensation, which runs into the hundreds. The gap has widened in recent times as CEO pay has soared and middle class compensation has stagnated and declined in real terms. Observers sometimes wonder why CEOs receive twice the pay of the next highest executive and see it as a sign of the United States becoming what economist Robert Frank has called a *winner-take-all* society.[26]

It's important for directors—who, after all, make executive compensation decisions—to be aware of these criticisms. They should also be aware of counterpoints. For example, a recent study[27] found that increases in company size almost entirely explain the increase in executive compensation in recent years. While CEO pay increased six-fold between 1980 and 2003, the market value of the companies they managed also increased six-fold over this period. Another study found that

> Growth in executive compensation is largely consistent with the growth in compensation for other highly paid professionals, such as hedge fund managers, venture capitalists, lawyers and professional athletes ... Pay among these groups all grew by roughly the same order of magnitude during 1994–2005.[28]

As an academic, I try hard to understand and evaluate all sides of the executive compensation debate. As a director, I am mindful of these perspectives, but board responsibility is clear: effective stewardship of one company. This means paying what is required (and not more) in a competitive marketplace to secure the talent needed to lead the company successfully.

Goals and Principles

The board's goals in designing executive compensation are

- to pay enough to attract and retain the executive talent needed to run the company well but not so much as to waste shareholder's resources;

- to design variable compensation so that executives do well financially if, and only if, pay is warranted by performance and, over time, shareholders do well; and

- to make the rest of compensation (perquisites and benefits) competitive but muted.

Participating in setting compensation for senior executives is a weighty responsibility. Over the last twenty-five years, I have developed insights and principles that guide my thinking:

- The goal is to secure the best possible value in engaging and compensating the organization's leaders. Be willing to pay top dollar for top talent, defined as achieving strong shareholder value creation over a sustained period and fulfilling the company's other purposes. Never give premium pay for mediocre results.

- It is much easier for executives to achieve strong short-term performance than to build enterprise value over the long term, so compensation should strongly reward the latter and not overly reward the former.

- In hard times, executives' pay should decline far more on both a dollar and percentage basis than most employees' because it rises far more in good times, and they can afford the hit.

- Be wary of golden handshakes because they commit a lot of shareholder money to executives who may or may not prove to be worth it. Avoid golden parachutes unless there is a compelling shareholder benefit.

- Use compensation consultants for benchmarking and expertise in plan design, but retain full control over compensation decisions.

- The entire board—not just the compensation committee— must understand and sign off on what and how the CEO and other senior people are paid. All will be held accountable by shareholders.

- Gut checks are important in compensation. Ask, "How will I feel about any possible outcome of what we are putting in place?" Some directors of the New York Stock Exchange claimed they didn't understand or realize what CEO Dick Grasso would ultimately be paid under plans they approved!

- Enable executives to become wealthy if, but only if, they make shareholders very wealthy and, in the process, build an organization with broad excellence that achieves high aspirations.

- Remember that much is expected in performance and commitment of those who are paid a lot. Don't hesitate to communicate this expectation to executives, and don't apologize for taking action when the expectation is not met.

A special risk directors need to guard against in compensation is back scratching between the CEO and directors. One form is a dominant CEO urging above-market compensation for directors. The CEO should have nothing whatsoever to do with director compensation, which is the province of the independent directors on the governance and compensation committees. Another risk is director interlock with CEOs serving on each other's boards and, in some cases, compensation committees. CEOs tend to sympathize with each other's challenges and what they believe constitutes appropriate pay for their troubles. Any such reciprocity is inappropriate.

Facts are friendly when making compensation decisions but only if they are comprehensive and balanced versus selective and purposeful. There is abundant information available publicly and from compensation consultants to help directors calibrate what their CEO and senior executives should be paid in base salaries, what their opportunities for bonuses relative to performance should be, and what the proper size of equity grants is. In addition, I find quite useful the compensation halls of fame and shame published in the media from time to time. They are a good reminder that some boards give away the store to executives with shareholders getting little in return. Other boards do it right, paying at a rate that attracts and retains talent who deliver outsized rewards to owners.

Ensure Quality Financial Reporting and Effective Internal Controls

Among the board's most important duties is ensuring that the organization's financial reporting is timely and accurate. This requires effective internal controls over the financial reporting process, which the board must also ensure.

It is impossible to be a responsible fiduciary without knowing with a high level of precision and significant amount of detail the organization's financial condition. In addition, owners and stakeholders have the right to know how the organization in which they have invested and placed their trust is performing. The purpose of financial reports is to serve the information needs of owners, directors, managers, and stakeholders.

The board's need to ensure quality financial reporting and effective internal controls is so important that an audit committee composed solely of independent directors, one of whom must be a financial expert and all of whom should be financially literate, is charged with this responsibility. Directors are more highly compensated for serving on the audit committee than on other committees, and rightly so. Being a conscientious member of the audit committee requires extensive preparation, reviewing hundreds of pages of financial reports, including mind-numbing but important footnotes, the Management Discussion and Analysis section of the annual report, myriad SEC filings, and the independent and internal auditor's plans and reports. It's a big job.

In my experience, two things matter most in directors discharging their duty to ensure quality financial reporting and internal controls. One is the competence, integrity, and direct access to the audit committee of the financial staff, especially the chief financial officer (CFO), chief accounting officer (CAO), and internal and independent auditors. The other is the vigilance and financial savvy of directors, especially but not exclusively those on the audit committee.

Financial Staff and Auditors

When I became president of the University of Illinois, I inherited from my predecessor a good group of senior executives. I found exactly what I expected in terms of roles and responsibilities with one exception: I looked in vain for the chief financial officer. I discovered, much to my surprise, that the university did not have a CFO. This was probably due to much of the university's funding coming from the state of Illinois for the first 120 years of its then 138-year history.

I was heading an institution with $4 billion in diverse revenue sources and complex spending requirements, billions in plant and equipment, and plenty of debt and other obligations. Though I had great respect for the person who headed administration and oversaw these activities, it unnerved me not to have an experienced financial expert on whom the board of trustees and I could rely to lead this critical function. I soon fixed the problem by recommending to the board the creation of a CFO position and recruiting an outstanding financial officer to fill it.

The point of the story is that the first thing a board must do to ensure quality financial reporting is satisfy itself that the senior executives directors are relying on to do the work are absolutely first class. It's playing with fire to have anything but the best in the CFO and CAO positions. They are the belt in the belt-and-suspenders of sound financial management. The auditors—internal and external—are the suspenders. The financial executives and auditors must know with certainty that they have *direct access* to the audit committee, especially its chair, on any matter about which they are concerned. Equally important, they must know that they are expected to *use that access* when circumstances warrant.

I have chaired audit committees, ensured a direct reporting line, and conveyed this expectation. The fact that it is infrequently used to report untoward activity does not mean that it is unimportant or ineffective. Rather, its main value is preventive. Even high integrity CEOs and CFOs can be tempted, under pressure for financial performance, to take actions that undermine the integrity of financial reporting. In the calculus of whether to do so or play straight, it helps for them to know that a committee of the board is focused on their decisions and is directly accessible by people with whom they work closely. For directors, the best problems are the ones that never occur.

Vigilance and Savvy

Accounting is the language of business. While introductory accounting can make it appear simple, financial statements of large enterprises are studies in complexity, and financial reports are far less precise than the numbers make them appear.

My CPA father pointed out to me years ago the paradox of expressing financial statement numbers down to the dollar even though uncertainty about the number can run to the millions.

Estimates, judgments, and reserves create wiggle room that allows management to *manage earnings*, and there is abundant academic evidence that many do. This can be a slippery slope leading to serious distortions in reported financial results, and managing earnings through accounting judgments is small potatoes compared to the outright deception and fraud that characterize most large-scale corporate meltdowns. It's important for directors to resist *schadenfreude* (taking pleasure in others' misery) when they read how boards failed to detect accounting practices that led to collapse or massive write-downs. A more appropriate reaction would be "there but for the grace of God go we!"

Directors should reflect on how such things happen. I think it starts with the deep human desire for things to be okay, especially when the people involved are beneficiaries of such conditions. How else to explain the ability of the Bernie Madoffs and Dennis Kozlowskis of the business world to fool so many people? One of the best lessons my dad taught me was to ask the question "Does this make sense?" If not, dig deeper. Did it really make sense for Bernie Madoff's investors to achieve steady, double-digit increases in the values of their portfolios for two decades while markets gyrated? Did it really make sense, given the decidedly mixed record of value creation for acquirers, for Tyco's reported earnings to grow steadily and its stock price to soar on the strength of over one hundred acquisitions in just a few years? More broadly, did it make sense for millions of Americans to participate in the mass fantasy that housing prices would increase in value at double-digit rates forever?

While directors should avoid being boardroom Cassandras, they must be vigilant and savvy about the realities of earnings management, deception, fraud, and the inevitability of what one good book calls manias, panics, and crashes.[29] These things occur with depressing regularity. Directors must be frontline sensing mechanisms and shutoff valves in such circumstances. Performing these roles effectively is essential to being a good steward and responsible fiduciary.

Oversee a Balance Sheet with Adequate Liquidity and Prudent Debt

Directors pay close attention to the income statement. They care about results, and period after period, the income statement reports those results—revenue, costs, gross margin, expenses, and net and af-ter-tax profit. To use a sports metaphor, the income statement reports management's stats on offense.

But directors should pay at least as much attention to the balance sheet. Continuing the sports metaphor, the balance sheet contains vital information on both financial bench strength and defensive staying power.

Companies get into serious trouble because of balance sheet weakness, far more than a period or two of weak earnings or losses. Most small companies fail because of undercapitalization—that is, inadequate cash to invest in the business. Larger companies get into trouble because of too little cash and too much debt. They lack the liquid reserves to meet payroll and pay bills and are unable to roll over or service their debt (make interest and principal payments).

A weak balance sheet is an invitation to trouble. By contrast, a strong balance sheet improves the odds that the board can maintain control over the company's destiny. It does not ensure a successful business and may even be too conservative to maximize sharehold-er value, but it does guarantee that the business will live to fight another day.

As an investor in Cummins' stock, here's the kind of commentary I like to read about the company:

> CMI's [Cummins] debt-to-equity ratio is very low at 0.13 and is currently below that of the industry average, implying that there has been very successful management of debt levels. Along with the favorable debt-to-equity ratio, the company maintains an adequate quick ratio [cash/equivalents + marketable securities + accounts receivable divided by current liabilities] of 1.13, which illustrates the ability to avoid short-term cash problems.[30]

Cummins' financial position is not right for every company, and perhaps it's too conservative for some people's taste. But it wouldn't be if they had worked in this highly cyclical capital goods industry like I did.

In my experience, the tastes of individual board members and executives vary widely when it comes to the balance sheet. My dad had a good way of describing this. "When it comes to debt," he said, "you have to decide if you want to eat well or sleep well." In other words, at one extreme are those who view plenty of debt as a smart way to leverage the capital base and increase return on investment. They may view bankruptcy as a legal and financial rather than a moral matter, just one more way to work out problems when they arise. At the other extreme are those who love cash, hate debt, and do all they can to maximize the former and minimize the latter.

Most business people have attitudes and practices somewhere in-between. They are comfortable, or learn to live, with just enough cash for liquidity needs and moderate debt to leverage their equity. Even so, they will work hard to make sure they are never truly strapped for cash or saddled with debt that is onerous in amount or terms. They tend to have a preference for borrowing that uses company assets (e.g., receivables and inventory) for collateral rather than putting the enterprise itself at risk.

Why do attitudes vary so widely on these important matters? I think it's because they are not just about financial management. Rather, they involve individuals' appetites and tolerances on deep issues, notably risk and control. The most successful entrepreneurs I know have a great penchant for control. Contrary to the gun-slinging, risk-loving image of entrepreneurs, they dislike debt because borrowing always means sharing control with someone outside the business. I would put the Gordon family in this category. While Paul and John borrowed money in the early stage of building Gordon Food Service, they viewed it as a necessary evil and have counseled subsequent generations away from excessive borrowing.

How does this penchant for control coexist with entrepreneurs' willingness to take risks? I think the answer is that for them, owning a business rather than working for someone else is the highest form of control. If taking risks to get there is required, they'll do it.

Note that when entrepreneurs borrow money, they put their own wealth at risk. Early on, borrowing may be in the form of credit card debt or a mortgage loan that can lead to personal bankruptcy if things go bad. Later, it is their business, or at least its assets, that are at risk.

It's different when public company executives borrow money (with board approval, of course). If they leverage up the company and things go well with successful acquisitions or new lines of business and plant and equipment, returns will be high and the stock price will benefit. They end up running a larger, more profitable enterprise that means larger salaries, bonuses, and stock incentives. If things go badly, it will be unpleasant. But unlike entrepreneurs, executives will not be forced into personal bankruptcy or lose a company they own and spent a lifetime building.

As a result, the risk/reward relationship for public company executives can tempt them to run debt up to a dangerously high level. The board, representing owners who get left holding the bag should things go wrong, should preemptively establish policies on acceptable debt levels based on stress test modeling of the company's financial performance through good times and bad. Then the board must enforce the policy, granting exceptions only for strategic reasons accompanied by a plan to return to the policy-prescribed debt level in an acceptable period of time.

My counsel to directors of both public and private companies is to carefully monitor the balance sheet. Resolve differences on the board about financial risk by creating a formal debt policy that is right for the company. The debt level should not, under arduous circumstances, put the company at mortal risk. Insist on generous liquidity relative to the company's needs over the business cycle. A strong balance sheet is just one element of managing enterprise risk.

Oversee Enterprise Risk

Only those who dare to fail greatly can ever achieve greatly.

—*Robert F. Kennedy*

To finish first, you must first finish.

—*Rick Mears, four-time Indy 500 winner*

The space between Kennedy's inspiring challenge and Mears's cautionary reminder is where directors must navigate a company on behalf of its owners and stakeholders. It's a tough assignment with substantial time lags between decisions taken today and future results. The stakes are high.

Take too little risk in a fast-changing, competitive world and a company will suffer poor performance and slow death. Take too much risk and the company will lose its independence, or worse, crash and burn.

Business is fundamentally about managing well in the face of powerful economic and financial forces: supply and demand and risk and return. The two are related. Excess supply and inadequate demand increase risk and depress returns; constrained supply and abundant demand reduce risk and increase returns. It is in this context that boards should approach their responsibility to oversee enterprise risk.

Business requires risk-taking. Public companies must disclose to investors the risks that could affect the business. I offer as evidence of the inevitability of risk in business the many pages in EQR's annual report listing the risks to which the company is exposed. They include normal business risks like cash flow, unique risks such as the need to re-let apartments when leases expire, the relative illiquidity of property assets, financial and stock market risks, and even climate change.

Management's job is to recognize and *mitigate* these risks to the extent economically feasible. It is the board's job to oversee the process and ensure the company's risk profile is such that

1. returns the company earns are commensurate with risks taken; and

2. the probability of *mortal risk* (dying or losing control of its destiny) is minimized.

Return earned for risk taken is the heart of business judgment. Minimizing mortal risk involves recognizing that while there may be discrete events that could destroy a company (e.g., asbestos health effects and resulting litigation), it is usually the *interaction among several risks* that brings companies down. The most obvious example, discussed in the previous section, is too much debt combined with too little liquidity intersecting with recessionary business conditions.

Enterprise risk management (ERM) has emerged since the 2008 financial crisis as an important responsibility performed by senior management and overseen by the board. It begins with a thorough risk assessment and documentation of mitigation strategies. Gaps are identified, and action is taken to fill them.

One of the best board risk assessments I have seen as a director is a framework consisting of four ranking categories (catastrophic, high, medium, and low) and a severity index relating risk categories to consequences (e.g., potential insolvency related to catastrophic risk, material decrease in earnings for high and medium risk, decrease in earnings and slow growth for low risk). In one company, over thirty enterprise risks were identified, described, and mapped into this framework. For each, a mitigation strategy was developed and implemented. It is an impressive piece of work that has left the organization less vulnerable to and far better prepared for risks that might materialize.

Preventing Slow Death

Author Jim Collins is best known for his books on business success, like *Good to Great* and *Built to Last*. But I think one of his lesser-known works, *How the Mighty Fall*, should be required reading for every director.[31] In it, he examines how once-successful companies end up on the trash heap of business history and compares them to peers who succeeded while facing similar circumstances. Especially useful for directors are the *stages of decline* that Collins chronicles:

- Hubris born of success
- Undisciplined pursuit of more
- Denial of risk and peril
- Grasping for salvation
- Capitulation to irrelevance or death

Collins asserts that this sequence is likely but not inevitable. The importance of the board serving as a circuit breaker in the death spiral is obvious.

Another book I would make required reading for directors is Clay Christensen's *The Innovator's Dilemma*.[32] Like Collins, Christensen examines how and why so many successful companies decline and become shadows of their former selves or die. He points to unintended consequences of companies' responses to low-cost competitors. Faced with lower cost competition, they try to protect profits by abandoning low-margin business. Their competitors chase them up the value chain. Ultimately, the previous industry leader yields too many lines of business and finds itself shrunken, weak, and irrelevant.

There is a popular—though I expect apocryphal—story among management gurus about the boiled frog. The gist of it is that if you throw a frog into a pan of boiling water, it will jump out and save itself, but if you put it in a pan of room-temperature water and turn up the heat, it will stay put and acclimate to the gradual rise in temperature until it boils to death. The reason it's a good story is that slow death appears to be a much more common cause of corporate mortality than sudden death. Collins and Christensen offer good insights about the slow death process and how to prevent it. This is, obviously, very useful knowledge for directors.

Enterprise Risk: A Searing Case Study

Let me conclude this section by relating an experience I had that that left an indelible impression about board responsibility for enterprise risk and mitigation. Put it under the heading of crisis management, an important topic for any board.

In 2001, I was a director of a family of mutual funds for which the Fred Alger Management firm was investment advisor. Fred Alger was a pioneer of the growth style of investing. Until Fred and a handful of other revolutionaries came along in the 1950s, the prevailing philosophy was to find a few good companies and buy and hold their stocks forever. The biggest and strongest were called widows' and orphans' stocks on the theory they were safe, secure, and permanent. Prominent among them were U.S. Steel and General Motors.

Fred was a brilliant investor who didn't buy conventional wisdom. He recognized that many successful companies have a finite period of rapid growth when much of their value is created. So rather than buy-and-hold, why not find such companies, get on at the bottom of their rapid growth escalators, capture the big increase in value, then get off at the top and do it all over again with different companies?

Fred was very successful. He was also, by most accounts, a personally conservative man. For example, Fred Alger Management, Inc. occupied the same modest offices on Maiden Lane in lower Manhattan for several decades until Fred's younger brother, David, became president of the firm.

David was expansive, optimistic, and a little flamboyant. In the 1990s, a great period for growth investing, he embodied that investing style, and the firm grew rapidly. The *New York Times* reported that when David took over the firm's operations in 1995, it had $3 billion in assets under management and 81 employees; in 2001 it had $15 billion in assets and 220 employees.[33]

Celebrating success, David moved the Alger firm's offices from Maiden Lane to the ninety-third floor of the North Tower of the World Trade Center. I recall the board meetings when I would arrive at the WTC, look up at those buildings, enter the lobby, join the crowd in a large, high-speed elevator, get off and transfer to another, smaller elevator, and emerge on the ninety-third floor to a spectacular sight. The Alger offices comprised a nearly unobstructed acre of modern, tasteful office furnishings, beyond which lay incredible views of Manhattan, the Statue of Liberty and Atlantic Ocean, the East River and Long Island, and the Hudson River and New Jersey.

David was immensely proud of his investing success, the growth and prosperity of the Alger firm, and their gorgeous new offices. We directors quickly learned that Fred had a different and ultimately prescient view.

At a board meeting, Fred declared that the WTC had been a marked building since the bombing there in 1993. He expressed his concern repeatedly even though most of the directors seemed to think—it's embarrassing to admit this now—that his concerns were overblown. Finally, Fred insisted that the firm mitigate the risk (not a term he or anyone else used) of being in the World Trade Center by creating a ready-to-function backup facility in northern New Jersey just in case. The cost was substantial, but Fred owned the majority of the firm, and his name was on the door. The board concurred, David complied, and it was done.

Good thing.

On the morning of September 11, 2001, the first plane to hit the World Trade Center at 8:48 am came in directly under the Alger offices. Everyone in the office at that time died tragically, including David Alger.

This tragedy could have been a mortal blow to Fred Alger Management. Instead, Fred and surviving members of the firm gathered as soon as they could—later that day as I recall—at the New Jersey backup office and began the work of rebuilding, even as they coped with shock and loss. Immediately, they reached out to reassure clients while continuing to manage portfolios. The firm survived.

David Alger's leadership reflected Bobby Kennedy's assertion that only those who dare to fail greatly can ever achieve greatly. This was his style in investing and in life. Fred Alger's leadership reflected Rick Mears's stern warning: you have to stay in the race to have a shot at winning. Both philosophies were required for Fred Alger Management to grow and prosper, then survive a near-death experience.

My takeaway as a director was that boards must recognize that both philosophies—the optimistic and exuberant, the sober and realistic—have a place in the enterprise risk management they oversee.

Be Vigilant about Investments, Especially Acquisitions and Mergers

Investments represent the big bets a company makes. By their nature, investments have a long life. The major ones have a profound impact on the business's success or failure. All investments affect a firm's financial returns because they are the denominator in return calculations. Because they are so consequential, a board needs to be sure that investments are prudent, then worked hard to generate return.

Management frequently proposes to grow or fill in missing elements of the product, technology, and capabilities lineup with an acquisition or, depending on the legal form of the business combination, a merger. This is always an interesting and exciting time for a board and senior management. Mergers and acquisitions (M&A) are strategy at work. The stakes can be high. Hardwired desires to capture and dominate come into play. The thrill of the chase is real.

This is also an excellent time for directors to be sober-minded. The board has two goals on behalf of shareholders: (1) grow the economic value of the firm over the long term, and (2) avoid putting the enterprise at mortal risk through excessive debt and other obligations. Will the proposed merger or acquisition contribute to the former? Is it consistent with the latter? These are the critical questions to which the board deserves honest and thoughtful answers from management.

Why do I urge sobriety when the party is most fun? Because the value creation history of acquisitions and mergers for acquiring companies is, overall, rather dismal. Research suggests that more often than not, M&A transactions destroy value for the acquiring company's shareholders while enhancing it for the selling company's. A recent study from the National Bureau of Economic Research (NBER) asserts that over the past 20 years, U.S. takeovers have led to losses of more than $200 billion for shareholders. The problem seems acute in large firms. They have destroyed $226 billion in shareholder wealth over that period while companies with bottom quartile capitalization created $8 billion through their transactions.[34]

Directors should remember that, occasionally, things go spectacularly wrong after apparently smart managers and diligent directors approve and execute big M&A deals. Consider, for example, Hewlett-Packard's $8.8 billion charge to earnings in November 2012, of which $5 billion was attributed to serious accounting improprieties at Autonomy, a British firm it acquired just a year earlier for $10 billion. Or Sprint's 2005 acquisition of Nextel for $36 billion and its subsequent write-down in 2008 of $29.7 billion. Or Daimler's $37 billion merger with Chrysler in 1998 followed by Daimler's sale of Chrysler to Cerberus Capital Management for $7 billion.

So directors shouldn't fall in love with M&A, but neither should they have a rigid aversion to it. Some are great successes. Think of Disney and Pixar, Sirius and XM, Exxon and Mobil, and other deals that were priced right, executed well, and brought together complementary capabilities, legally reduced competition, and improved efficiencies through scale.

M&A transactions can grow or destroy value. Directors can be most helpful in maximizing the former and minimizing the latter by asking hard questions and creating constructive tension with management as deals are debated. Here are some critical questions for directors to ask before signing off on a proposed merger or acquisition:

- Does it make strategic sense? Will it create value for shareholders over the long term?

- What is the true, total cost of the transaction including

not only purchase price but also required post-transaction investments and, possibly, funding losses?

- What are alternative strategic uses of capital (e.g., invest in growing the business organically), and are any of them better than the proposed transaction?

- Will the target be integrated into the acquirer and if so, are the social issues (e.g., cultural compatibility) such that this will be feasible? Or will the approach be like Berkshire Hathaway's in which current owners and managers will continue to lead the business with a high level of autonomy?

- How will the deal be funded, what will be the effect on the company's balance sheet, and is the resulting risk level acceptable?

- Will integration of the acquisition divert resources from work and investments required to continue to be successful in the base business?

- Has management fallen in love with the deal or succumbed to the thrill of the chase such that they are willing to pay an inflated price or present overly optimistic projections of future value?

- Could the transaction put the company at mortal risk? Remember that the recent Great Recession created business conditions for many companies that were two to three times worse than the worst case they had built into their business models.

Since M&A transactions can be so consequential for a company, it is important for directors to know the legal context in which they are making decisions. The general counsel will remind the board to

- exercise their fiduciary duties—that is, act in good faith, in the best interests of the company, and with the care of an ordinarily prudent person;

- rely on the business judgment rule, a judicial presumption that the board acted in accordance with the statutory standard of conduct reflected in the board's reliance on information from officers and advisors and its careful, educated, and well-advised decision process; and

- act only if they believe doing so is in the best long-term interests of the company and the shareholders in aggregate.

Assist Management in Uniquely Useful Ways

Recall that the board has two roles vis-à-vis management: to monitor and assist. The proper motto when it comes to monitoring is *trust but verify*. The proper motto when it comes to assisting is *facilitate but don't rush*.

Senior management is a high-energy, high-pressure game in which the goal is to grow value. Many actions are required to do so. The board can help management by moving along those matters that require board input or approval, of which there are many. A board that *unnecessarily* slows the decision process deflates management. If that is the board's intention, it should fire the current executives and put in place ones they can support.

I emphasize *unnecessarily* because there are issues on which a good board does slow the process. That's when directors and management are not on the same page or, more commonly, when the board simply doesn't have the information, analysis, and comfort required to be good fiduciaries. Then directors are obliged *not* to proceed but be clear with management about what will be required in the way of substance and process to enable them to make an informed judgment.

Beyond moving things along, it is sometimes difficult for directors to add value to a highly competent management team. They are full time while the board is part time. They are experts in the organization's business and industry; directors may or may not be.

Indeed, it's often difficult for a director even to *know* if he or she is adding value. Maze-bright executives know the best management responses to directors are phrases like *great point* and *excellent question*, which may or not be true. I don't recall an executive ever saying to a director, "We already covered that, weren't you listening?" or "What a dumb question!" even though everyone in the room was thinking it.

Because directors want to and can be helpful to management, here are a few guiding thoughts on the subject.

First, remember the difference between governing and managing. Directors are not members of the management team. It's not their job to have initiatives on which they are following up and checking progress except in domains for which the board is responsible, like executive compensation. Directors should focus on strategy, the annual operating plan and long-range plan, results against plan, and effectiveness of the leadership team. Directors are entitled, indeed obliged, to satisfy themselves about financial strength and the quality and integrity of financial reporting. When anything of consequence doesn't smell right to a director, he should ask questions until satisfied that it was a false alarm or there is a problem that is being satisfactorily addressed.

Second, *how* directors assist management really matters. For example:

- When something consequential is on a director's mind, it's helpful to discuss it with at least one other director before taking it to management. Well-considered ideas, questions, and concerns are preferable to those that are top-of-mind or shoot-from-the-hip.

- With management, a director's presumptive first stop is always the CEO. As noted earlier, unity of command (a single line of authority) is an important management principle, nowhere more than at the top of the organization. Board behavior should reinforce, not undermine, the authority of the CEO. This sets the stage for the board's holding the CEO accountable for results.

- Asking questions is a director's most effective way of exercising influence. Invariably, the best directors are those who ask the best questions. Good questions lead management and other directors to think and consider. They spur useful conversation. They plant ideas. Eminent academic Ed Schein's book *Humble Inquiry* is deeply instructive on how to ask questions well.[35]

- Henry Schacht, Cummins' chairman, taught me the value of asking "How do you know?" when someone makes a consequential but unsupported assertion. For example, if an executive says, "I'm confident we can launch this product at this price without provoking a destructive response from the competition," and a director has doubts about it, requiring an answer to "How do you know?" will make apparent the strength or weakness of the executive's position.

Third, because it really is lonely at the top, a compliment or word of encouragement, especially when the going is tough, can make a world of difference to senior executives. So can perspective, as in "Look, this is a big deal. Are we treating it as such?" or "This is important but it won't make or break the company" or "Are you, perhaps, a little more worked up than warranted by the matter at hand?" It's also wise and humane to remember that executives, like other employees, have lives beyond work, to acknowledge their joys and sorrows and to be supportive when they need it most.

Finally, the board through the lead director or individual directors on their own initiative can often deliver the greatest value by simply saying to the CEO and others, "How can we help?" The answers can be surprising. "By continuing to support our direction while we get through this rough patch," or "Would you talk with Nancy? Something seems amiss with her, she's critical to the management team and I'd appreciate a second opinion," or "I'd really like to know what's on the board's mind right now. Let's have a dinner of only the board and me so I can listen to each of you." It's easy—but often wrong—to presume to know how directors can best assist management. It helps just to ask.

Renew the Board

A stale board is incapable of delivering great governance, and it's easy for a board to grow stale. Directors can come to view their positions as sinecures and gradually get more and more comfortable depending on the CEO and management to run the business with only superficial oversight. Management dominates the board while acting deferential, pleasing and flattering directors with excellent pay, meals, accommodations, and trips. Meetings are pleasant. Camaraderie is high. Conflict is low. Everyone is happy—until a major problem occurs.

There are three antidotes to a board's going stale:

- Evaluation
- Education
- Renovation

Evaluation

An annual board evaluation is critical to keeping the board and its members fresh. At EQR, the governance committee that I chair manages this process. Sometimes it's written; sometimes I interview each trustee.

When we do written evaluations, trustees receive two forms: one to evaluate the board, the other to evaluate individual trustees. The latter includes a self-evaluation. We have used the same forms for several years to allow year-over-year comparison of responses and then change the forms to keep the process fresh.

Trustees complete the evaluation forms—some electronically, some hardcopy, it's their choice—and return them to me as chair of the governance committee. I tally the results. Alternatively, I interview trustees and ask for their evaluation of board, committee, and individual trustees' performance as well as ideas for improvement. At the March governance committee and board meetings,

I distribute the board self-evaluation results, and we discuss reported strengths, weaknesses, and ideas for improvement. This has resulted in many useful changes over the years in the way the board operates, such as the use of executive sessions, scheduling of committee meetings, and design of board dinners (with and without management and even the configuration of tables to facilitate productive discussion).

I share with each trustee summaries of peer evaluations of him or her. Trustees are very candid in evaluating their colleagues. Over the years, every trustee, including the chairman and the CEO, has received feedback that reinforces strengths and highlights weaknesses and specifies ways in which he or she can contribute more to the board. Examples to various trustees: "Be a better listener, don't dominate the discussion." "You know so much about the business, we need to hear more from you." "Be sure you're devoting the time required to the board." "Make your points more succinctly."

I have seen data suggesting that over three-fourths of public company boards now do a board self-evaluation annually. That's good, but fewer than half reportedly conduct an annual peer evaluation. This is definitely low-hanging fruit when it comes to director effectiveness.

Education

Because I am a professor and career-long educator, it's not surprising that I believe directors benefit greatly from education. This includes regularly reading the quality business press, such as the *Wall Street Journal, Financial Times*, and *The Economist*. It also includes in-person executive programs offered to directors by organizations like the National Association of Corporate Directors and top business schools.

Peer evaluation sometimes points to deficiencies that individual directors should correct though education. The most frequent, in my experience, is financial literacy. If a director is inadequately versed in financial statement analysis and accounting conventions, a quality *finance for non-financial managers* program is highly recommended.

Some board education should be done as a group. An idea from EQR's board self-evaluation several years ago was to have management periodically give us an in-depth presentation on some aspect of our business that is not normally covered in the board's agenda. We've had sessions on trends in apartment living, social media, and property development as well as visits to properties in various cities.

It is essential for a board and individual directors to invest in their intellectual capital and keep themselves fresh.

Renovation

No matter how good its evaluation and education processes, every board needs fresh infusions of talent from time-to-time. New people on a board bring new ideas and shake up the status quo, including roles, alliances, and even seating (most directors are extreme creatures of habit when it comes to where they sit at the board table).

Opinions and practices vary about how to ensure that board members don't serve beyond their shelf life. Some boards have a mandatory retirement age; fewer have term limits. In my experience there are problems with both. Boards sometimes make exceptions so that directors can serve past the mandatory retirement age, suggesting that age is not a very good predictor of value. Term limits are an even blunter instrument, mandating departure from the board of directors who may be at peak value.

I think the best approach is a quality director evaluation and feedback process along with firm guidance, when needed, about the need for a director to retire from the board. The directors I admire most have charted their own courses when it came time for retirement from the board. When they thought they had served long enough, they simply informed the board with plenty of lead time to allow for orderly succession, then retired of their own accord with abundant expressions of appreciation from their colleagues.

The chairman, lead director, and governance committee should be attentive to the layering of the board in terms of ages, career stages, and length of board service. These factors, together with the results of annual board and director evaluations, can guide judgments about when directors should leave the board. In recruiting new directors, the goal is to fill out the portfolio of profiles (experiences, industries, expertise, and diversity of all kinds) needed for a high-functioning board.

Timing is an important consideration in board turnover. It is important to avoid too many moving parts at any one time in the senior ranks. Thus, it's preferable for directors to leave when the organization is performing well. Things get very busy when times are bad, and director departures can inadvertently signal distress to employees, investors, and other constituents.

I have often told managers that it's important to take care of themselves physically, mentally, and psychologically because they can't lead others effectively unless they are fit, sharp, and centered. The equivalent advice for boards is that they must constantly self-renew because great governance requires directors who are alert, attentive, and on top of their game. The best way to achieve this is through regular board evaluation, education, and renovation.

Conclusion

In this chapter, I've reported on the "top ten plus one" things that constitute the vital substance of board work. I've discussed why they are important and offered ideas on how to go about them.

Doing the right things is essential, but directors must also do things right—the subject to which we turn next.

CHAPTER 5

Do Things Right

The Process of Great Governance

A board is a work group—senior, consequential, and privileged—but a work group nonetheless. As such, the determinants of its effectiveness are well known: people, structure, and process.

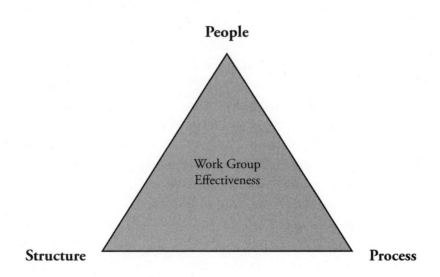

Directors themselves are surely the most important determinant of board effectiveness. Dean Gilbert R. Whitaker Jr., my boss at the University of Michigan, once remarked that if you have a great faculty, they attract great students. Gather them together under a tree and great education will occur. In general, I think the same is true of boards. Great directors will, most of the time, be good stewards, whatever the board's structure and process.

How important is the human makeup of the board? The late J. Richard Hackman, arguably the world's leading expert on teams, advised that individuals destructive to a group's work process literally must be forced off. I have certainly found this is true on boards. Hackman came to other conclusions that board chairs, lead directors, and governance committees should keep in mind. For example, small teams are generally more effective than large ones; he suggests no more than nine members. Stable and experienced teams are more effective than those newly formed or comprising many new members; this should give pause about mandatory retirement based on term limits or age. Deviants (members with critical and different perspectives) are important to challenging the team's tendency toward homogeneity.[36]

Still, we can't rely on boards comprising only great directors, and there are too many instances in which well-qualified directors have overseen (or overlooked) circumstances that led to disastrous results.

Structure always matters. Variables such as board size, committees, and leadership roles deserve attention, but as we will see in the next chapter, research relating board structure to effectiveness as measured by organizational performance is disappointingly equivocal in its findings.

If structure is important but inconclusive when it comes to board effectiveness and great directors are highly desirable but not a guarantee of great governance, we are left to consider *process* as a critical determinant of governance success. By process, I mean *how individual directors and the board as a whole go about their work.*

Process Basics

Board process is a difficult subject because it is invisible except to the participants, and most boards meet privately. Allow me to draw on my experience as a director to offer two top-ten lists of process basics.

Process Advice for Individual Directors

1. **Prepare.** Read meeting materials, identify issues for clarification and discussion, and come with questions and comments.

2. **Attend.** There is no substitute for in-person attendance.

3. **Participate.** Make value-added contributions.

4. **Initiate.** Raise consequential issues for consideration.

5. **Be diligent.** Work hard to understand the company's mission, strategy, plan, and performance as well as its financial position, people, and culture.

6. **Be financially literate.** Learn enough accounting because it is the language of business.

7. **Be both tough and helpful.** Maintain high standards, don't tolerate poor performance, assist in solving problems, and be supportive.

8. **Be constructive.** The goal is to get the work of the board and the company done, not win arguments.

9. **Be candid and courageous.** It's a director's fiduciary duty and your goal is respect, not popularity.

10. **Don't** meddle, dominate, engage in ego contests with other directors, or stay too long.

Process Advice for the Board

1. **Elect and appoint leaders (chairman, CEO, lead director, committee chairs) who are strong and inclusive.**

Maintain unity of command: the board is accountable to shareholders, CEO to the board, management to the CEO.

2. **Design agendas—annual and for each meeting—to ensure vital business gets done while leaving white space** for matters arising and discussion.

3. **Delegate but don't abdicate** to board committees.

4. **Decide on the board's information needs** and require management to meet them.

5. **Insist on excellent staff work** to support the board.

6. **Act with a sense of urgency**, but deliberate important matters as long as necessary.

7. **Have a good mix of meetings** with management present and executive sessions of directors and independent directors only.

8. **Get out of the boardroom** occasionally: hit the road to observe, learn, and show the flag.

9. **Combat staleness** with education sessions, board and director evaluations and feedback, and planned turnover and succession.

10. **Don't** meddle, play politics, tolerate an incompetent director or executive, or ignore smoke (there's usually a fire).

These process basics are time-tested and essential. However, they guarantee neither great results nor avoidance of disaster. Deeper insight is required.

Digging Deeper on Board Process

This book's starting point was the story of two companies that have had striking success since they created formal governance arrangements over two decades ago: Gordon Food Service in 1988 and Equity Residential in 1993. Directors deeply desire that the companies they govern thrive on their watch. I can report from personal experience that it's gratifying when this occurs.

Thriving is the hoped-for condition, but an essential pre-condition to thriving is *surviving*. This means avoiding catastrophic losses and setbacks. Great governance requires a board process that maximizes the probability of the company or organization both surviving and thriving.

What are the process requirements for this to occur? In my experience, *the boardroom must be a place of good information, rational analysis, quality discourse, careful consideration, and wise judgment.* This requires directors who are intent on perceiving, thinking, and working this way and a process that facilitates it. My purpose in this chapter is to convey what I know, suspect, and believe about boardroom process that can result in great governance. My views are informed by experience along with insights from behavioral research that are transforming the fields of economic, finance, and accounting.

I had a remarkable intellectual experience while doing research for this book and teaching a course on corporate governance at the University of Illinois. The textbook for the course was *Corporate Governance Matters* (CGM)[37] by David Larcker and Brian Tayan of the Corporate Governance Research Program at the Stanford Graduate Business School. *CGM* is an excellent compendium of empirical research, primarily from finance and accounting, on the relationship between many governance variables, mainly structural (e.g., board size, whether chairman and CEO are combined or separate, the independence of directors, etc.), and the financial performance of the companies being governed. The results of this research can only be called disappointing, which the authors admirably acknowledge.

While I taught the course and absorbed *CGM*, I also read *Thinking Fast and Slow*,[38] an impressive exposition of the findings and implications of behavioral research by Daniel Kahneman. Kahneman is a Princeton psychologist who won the Nobel Prize in Economics in 2002 for his conceptual work and experimental research with a late colleague, Amos Tversky. Insights from their work have challenged the long-standing *rational man* assumption of economics. Kahneman was the first non-economist to win the Nobel Prize in Economics.

I found that *CGM*, a book about governance, offered me relatively few insights as a corporate and nonprofit director on how to improve governance due to the equivocal nature of the research findings on which it reports. By contrast, *Thinking Fast and Slow*, which has nothing explicitly to do with governance, was rich with insight and useful ideas! Why? Because while the research variables in *CGM* are primarily structural and among the least important in affecting board performance, the variables in *Thinking Fast and Slow* involve people and process: perception, cognition, bias, and the consequences for how individuals and groups work and make decisions. These are the elements of board process that most affect governance effectiveness. Allow me to illustrate.

Individual and Organizational Dynamics

An influential book I read as a young man was *The Best and The Brightest* by the late journalist David Halberstam.[39] It is a riveting account of how some of the most talented men of the post–World War II era led the United States into the Vietnam War, then repeatedly doubled down until a humiliating defeat ended the nightmare. Hundreds of thousands of lives were lost, including 58,000 Americans. Billions in treasure were expended, and confidence in the veracity and competence of government was permanently shaken. The book instilled in me a career-long fascination with senior-level decision-making and an acute awareness that smart and able people, with the best of intentions, can make terrible decisions. Halberstarm's account of President Lyndon B. Johnson, Secretary of State Dean Rusk, Secretary of Defense Robert S. McNamara, General William Westmoreland, and others planted two ideas firmly in my mind:

1. Individuals have preconceptions and preferences, rooted in their personal histories, that deeply affect perceptions, create biases, and influence judgments in ways of which they are largely unaware.

2. The organizational context in which leaders operate can distort the information on which they rely and amplify their biases in decision-making, rendering them isolated and dependent.

Individual Dynamics. The first insight—about individuals' preconceptions and preferences and their consequences—has been reinforced for me in thirty years of senior management and board experience. *The Best and the Brightest* offers unforgettable illustrations. Here's one of them.

Rusk and McNamara were hawks who fought doves like McGeorge Bundy (Johnson's National Security Advisor) to influence Johnson on war policy. According to Halberstam, they learned to present tactical alternatives to Johnson (e.g., on strategies for bombing the north) with their preferred course of action placed squarely in the middle of two extreme options, creating the impression that it was the moderate or prudent option. This played well to Johnson, who was torn over war policy. Reluctant to escalate enough to win (if winning was possible) but unwilling to "turn tail," Johnson was drawn to the middle course. As a result, Rusk and McNamara usually got their way. This led over time to a gradual but vast escalation in the war which would undoubtedly have appalled Johnson had it been presented in a single plan.

Thanks to behavioral research, the effects of such *framing* on perception and decision bias are far better understood now than then. Another phenomenon on which such research has shed light is *anchoring*. It played a big role in Vietnam War decision-making. Johnson and his contemporaries were steeped (anchored) in lessons from World War II and the Korean and Cold Wars. The lessons were that aggression must be stopped or it will escalate into broad domination and expanded conflict, and Communism is an aggressive and expansionary international force.

When these leaders looked at the situation in Vietnam in the 1960s, they saw, analogously, Germany and Poland in 1939, the Soviet Union and Eastern Europe following World War II, and China and South Korea in 1950. As they tried to make sense of what was happening (sense-making is a much-studied behavioral concept),

what Kahneman calls their System 1 (fast) thinking kicked in immediately to give them guidance: *Communist aggression must be stopped.*
Those opposed to the war suggested alternative anchoring (e.g., Ho
Chi Minh as the George Washington of Vietnam, fighting for freedom.) But they were derided, illustrating another behavioral concept
that affects perception and judgment: the recency effect. When asked
to recall a list of items in any order (free recall), people tend to begin
with the end of the list, recalling those items best. Thus, more recent
events (like international Communism) likely had a larger anchoring
effect than those in the distant past (like the American Revolution).

These illustrations demonstrate the profound ways in which
framing, anchoring, bias, and types of thinking can affect judgment.
Here is another, much simpler example I've used with my students.

Like most people, I drive exactly the same route to work every
day. One morning recently, I saw that my usual route was blocked
due to road construction. So instead of going east, south, and east
again to get to the parking lot, I went east, *north* then east again.
After my second turn to go east, I came, as usual, to a stop sign at
the road I always cross, but this time a few blocks north. I stopped,
looked both ways, then proceeded … and immediately hit an oncoming car. (It was a low-speed impact, and, fortunately no one was
hurt.) Why? Because on my usual route, the intersection is a *four-way*
stop, while the intersection to the north is *two-way*. Only I had to
stop. The oncoming traffic had the right of way.

My mind was engaged in Kahneman's System 1 (fast) thinking, and why not? I have commuted to work hundreds of times.
On mental autopilot, I proceeded on the usual assumption that the
oncoming cars would stop. Nothing about the situation triggered
Kahneman's System 2 (slow, careful, deliberate) thinking. If it had,
I would have been more aware, considered, and careful, recognizing
that, appearances to the contrary, this situation was novel and the
risk level was elevated.

I have reflected that had my wife been with me, I probably would
have avoided the accident. Why? First, I'm more watchful and careful
when driving with others for reasons of pride and safety. Second,
there would have been two brains at work on the matter instead of

one. (I don't want to say that my wife doesn't trust my driving, but she doesn't. So she pays attention and alerts me.) Two or more minds often are better than one.

Surely this is a reason that commercial airliners always have two pilots and why juries rather than judges alone determine guilt versus innocence in criminal matters. (Watch the classic Henry Fonda film *Twelve Angry Men* with this in mind.) This is why CEOs (individuals) report to boards (groups) in all public companies and, by choice, in many private companies as well.

These practices result from our understanding that the perceptions and mental processes of one individual are more likely to lead to faulty decisions than the multiple perceptions and mental processes of a group that deliberates and decides together. While there is evidence that groups, *on average*, make better decisions than individuals, the process is not automatic, as Halberstam illustrates in *The Best and the Brightest*. The group needs a diversity of perceptions and perspectives and a process to bring them together to produce good decisions. This is certainly the case for boards.

Organizational Dynamics. Boards must concern themselves not only with matters that affect individual perception and judgment but also with organizational dynamics that can affect directors' decision-making. Two risks are noteworthy in this regard.

First is the quality of information on which directors rely. Most boards have some version of a dashboard (a visual summary) of results that supports their monitoring duty. But how reliable are the gauges? In *The Best and the Brightest*, Halberstam describes the hazards leaders faced through the paradox in Vietnam of the United States supposedly winning battles and body counts by overwhelming margins while consistently losing the war. Pressures and incentives for performance in the U.S. military and Foreign Service led to selective and inflated reporting and optimistic interpretation of results (i.e., gauges with faulty readings).

In this vein, I once had a direct report who had a bad habit of beginning every meeting with "Joe, I have some good news for you!" It made me uneasy.

After a while, I said to him, "That's great, but why don't you tell me *first* the things you're concerned about since we're here to solve problems. Then if there's time for good news at the end, fine, or you can just shoot me an e-mail." It was my way of encouraging more balanced and less selective reporting of what was going on in his area of responsibility.

The second risk of which directors must be aware is the tendency of organizations and their leaders to fall in love with courses of action that may not be optimal or wise. Acquisitions and mergers are a prime example, as discussed previously. This helps explain their overall poor record of value creation for the acquirer. Here's another example: the high bay stacker.

Inventory management is a big issue in every manufacturing company. It was at Cummins when I worked there. Inventory matters because if there's too much, it's expensive and wasteful, but if there is too little or the wrong kind, it costs sales and hurts customer service. There has been a sea change in attitudes about manufacturing inventory in recent decades, from *manage it well* to *minimize it*. The change has been driven by the shareholder value and quality movements and facilitated by information technology and transportation systems.

When I joined Cummins, there was a lot of talk about a proposed high bay stacker for the Walesboro, Indiana, components plant that machined parts for Cummins engines that were assembled a few miles away in Columbus and elsewhere. This piqued my curiosity. I learned that the stacker was a multi-million dollar physical system in combination with a sophisticated information system to accommodate (stack) inventory by using air space (high) in one section (bay) of the plant. The stacker would accommodate far more in-process inventory than normal floor storage. In those days, manufacturing's view was *the more inventory, the better*. Abundant inventory helped smooth production and minimize stock-outs that disappointed customers and distributors. The manufacturing organization had fallen in love with the high bay stacker concept and pushed Jim Henderson, the president, to secure board approval for the multi-million dollar capital investment.

Jim appeared ready to agree but then held off. Tension grew. Ultimately, manufacturing management did not get their heart's desire. The president insisted on a fundamental change in manufacturing *thinking* about inventory. Too much of it was not only costly, it also undermined quality by serving as a crutch when defective parts couldn't be used by the assembly line. Instead of storing more inventory efficiently, Jim established a goal of drastically reducing inventory through high-quality, lean production and just-in-time delivery of components to the assembly line. Manufacturing was not happy, but it's clear, in retrospect, that the president was right.

Boards and executives must be alert that organizations do, indeed, fall in love with ideas and initiatives. Powerful momentum develops behind proposals requiring their approval. Succumbing is the course of least resistance. Doing so minimizes conflict and makes people happy, at least in the short term, but it's not always the right thing to do.

There are organizational dynamics beyond distorted reporting and falling in love with initiatives that impair board decision-making. Functional dominance can be a problem. For example, finance organizations became too powerful relative to design (product) and manufacturing (cost and quality) in U.S. auto companies, contributing to decades of decline. Financial incentives that are too weak, too strong, or poorly targeted can also cause trouble. This may explain the infamous statement by Charles O. Prince, then CEO of Citigroup, in mid-2007 at the peak of the financial bubble. Explaining the company's aggressive lending to private equity for leveraged buyout deals at nosebleed prices, he said, "As long as the music is playing, you've got to get up and dance. We're still dancing."[40] The lending produced enormous fees that bulked up profits on which annual bonuses were based. Shareholders and taxpayers were left holding the bag when loans soured.

Wise boards need to be attentive and on guard about the effects on major decisions of these and other organizational dynamics.

Behavioral Research

Economists used to assume that human actors are rational and omniscient and, therefore, able to make unbiased decisions based on complete information and objective reasoning to maximize their *utility*. This simplified and simplistic view of human beings led to the notion of markets as perfect, with prices the result of millions of decisions accurately reflecting all relevant information, adjusted instantly and continuously.

These assumptions may be convenient for economic analysis, but they don't square with the decision processes of real human beings. Our decisions are subject to emotions and biases, inaccurate perceptions, ignorance, and misinformation. A perfect markets view doesn't square with the obvious manic-depressive character of markets at times and their tendency toward excesses like bubbles and busts. Yet the assumptions persisted in economic analysis for a long time because of inertia, the benefits of simplification in modeling, and the lack of a well-grounded alternative. Gradually, though, things have changed. Thanks to scholars like Kahneman and Tversky, we now have a richer understanding of how people perceive and process information and make decisions. In the real world, directors and executives can be much more aware of impediments to the boardroom being a place of good information, rational analysis, quality discourse, careful consideration, and wise judgment. Foremost among the impediments are bounded rationality and motivated reasoning.

Bounded Rationality. One of the first scholars to question the omniscient, rational man assumption and offer a useful alternative was Herbert Simon, an organizational scholar who articulated the concept of *bounded rationality*.[41] Simon concluded after examining executive decision-making that people are not hyper-rational supermen and superwomen with unlimited deductive ability assumed by traditional economic models.

Rather, there are serious limits (bounds) to their rationality. This leads them to use simplifying assumptions and decision rules that we now call *heuristics* when making judgments and decisions. Many heuristics are useful and necessary, allowing us to conserve scarce cognitive resources. One scholar refers to most human information processing as *fast and frugal*.[42] But heuristics can lead to errors and unintended biases, as illustrated by examples of Vietnam War decision-making in *The Best and the Brightest* and my judgment error in a novel situation that led to an auto accident.

I have noted in this book the importance of financial statements in enabling boards to monitor management and evaluate performance. Flowing directly from bounded rationality is a large stream of literature on *format effects* in financial reporting, which finds that more saliently displayed information receives more attention and is weighted more heavily in judgments and decisions. For example, one study[43] found that explicitly disclosing information (e.g., in an earnings announcement or press release) improves market efficiency, even when these disclosures are redundant. In other words, just repackaging value-relevant information that is already available and highlighting it can improve market efficiency.

In similar fashion, experienced directors know that *how* management presents financial information to them can have a powerful effect on their perception of performance. Research shows that we subconsciously pay attention to information that is presented more prominently, but the most prominent information may not be the most important.

Bounded rationality reminds directors that neither they nor management can know and process all relevant information, even on important issues. This is why the best directors ask questions much more frequently than they give answers or make declarations. Questions open pathways and can bring new information and considerations to bear on consequential matters. "Have you thought about x, y or z?" is an excellent governance question for this reason.

In retrospect, I think that Irwin Miller at Cummins was making reference to the problem of bounded rationality when he once said to me, "In management, you don't have to worry about what you already know. You're working on it. Worry about what you *don't* know." This is true for directors as well.

Motivated Reasoning. Encouraged by the pioneering work of Herbert Simon and his Nobel Prize in Economics in 1978, intellectually adventurous scholars in economics, finance, and accounting began to examine the findings of experimental psychologists and consider what the insights might mean for their own research. The results have been transforming these fields for the last two decades.

The most important finding of which directors should be aware is the concept of *motivated reasoning*. It occurs frequently in boardrooms and may explain better than anything else how and why groups of smart people can make inferior and occasionally truly awful decisions.

While bounded rationality establishes that we are unable to process all available information, subsequent research has established that we selectively search for and process available information that supports our preferences and goals. This is motivated reasoning: *analysis based on selective versus unbiased information and weighting that information in ways that lead to decisions consistent with our goals and preferences.*

We know that individuals have preferences and goals and that these are deeply rooted in their psyches. For example, looking at the same information, the majority of white Americans were convinced that O.J. Simpson was guilty of murder, while the majority of African-Americans believed he was innocent and concurred with the *not guilty* verdict.[44]

Motivated reasoning is a generalized bias to which we are all susceptible. When information is consistent with our preferences, we tend to accept it at face value and don't search for contradictory evidence. But when information is not consistent with our preferences, we actively scrutinize and attempt to discredit it. This happens even though we think we are being objective. For example, one scholar found that investors in long stock positions forecast higher earnings than investors in short positions when given identical information.[45] (A long position benefits from a higher future stock price, and a short position benefits from a lower price and earnings presumably drive prices.) In this context, it's easy to see why a board hungry for top-line growth could be persuaded to make a big acquisition at an inflated price, especially when management musters selective evidence to support the action and price.

Here's a boardroom-relevant example of motivated reasoning from *Thinking Fast and Slow*: "He likes the project, so he thinks its costs are low and its benefits are high. Nice example of the affect heuristic." The *affect heuristic* means that the individual is influenced in decision-making by his feelings about the project, something we've all observed and experienced.

Motivated reasoning can occur in important personnel decisions, such as hiring a CEO or evaluating candidates for the board. I remember being shocked when I first read research on the employment interviewing process, which found that subjective impressions in the first few minutes of an interview lead the interviewer to have a positive or negative disposition toward the candidate, which she then spends the remainder of the interview reinforcing with selective solicitation and interpretation of facts. I've certainly seen this happen in CEO and director interviews. This is not to say that chemistry doesn't matter; people have to like and respect each other well enough to work together. But motivated reasoning in this context can lead to problems, such as excessive emphasis on weaknesses in internal candidates the board knows well and too much emphasis on positive attributes and glossing over shortcomings of outside candidates.

Another form of motivated reasoning is found in the *self-serving attribution bias*. When things go right, we attribute the success to our talent and hard work, but when they go wrong, we attribute the failure to things beyond our control such as the situation or bad luck. I've observed that golfers tend to claim ownership of their pars and birdies, feeling they are a proper reward for skill, practice, and persistence, but they often disclaim bad shots, holes, and rounds, attributing them to distractions, a new swing or anything but their own ineptitude

Self-serving attribution bias is often at work in the boardroom. When results are good, management and the board tend to take credit. When results are poor, management may point to factors beyond their control (e.g., the economy, the weather, or irrational competition). Right or wrong, good results don't require much explanation. Boards and management accept them as confirmation of their judgment and skill. Poor results, however, unleash rationales.

Recent research suggests that even experienced financial managers—professionals on whom boards rely for accurate scorekeeping
and even-handed interpretation of results—give greater weight to
internal than external factors in explaining past good performance.[46]
This leads them to be overconfident in future performance and more
likely to issue optimistic forecasts.

The self-serving attribution bias poses a challenge for governance. A great board gives credit where it's due for good results and
accepts valid rationales for poor results. But directors also understand
that luck and factors beyond management's control play a role in
both cases. Only the *pattern of performance compared to the competition* over a sustained period really tells the story of how management
is doing.

The bottom line for directors on motivated reasoning is that we
humans search for and process information in ways that support our
preferences and goals as well as our view of ourselves as smart, good
performers. We screen out or rationalize information that is incompatible with this view. Whether practiced by management and accepted by the board or practiced by the board itself, these tendencies
can seriously undermine the objectivity and rationality required for
directors to make wise decisions and accurately evaluate performance.

System 1 and System 2. Central to Kahneman's work in *Thinking
Fast and Slow* are the System 1 and System 2 constructs. System 1
thinking is fast. It is how we make most day-to-day decisions and
involves intuitive judgments and preferences. System 2 thinking is
slow, what Kahneman calls *a more deliberate mode of operation.*

Every director can relate to these constructs. Much of the time,
directors must process information quickly and make judgments intuitively, based on long experience. This is System 1 thinking. As
Kahneman observes, "Most behavior is intuitive, skilled, unproblem-
atic and successful." It suffices and gets the job done. A key issue
for directors is when and for what a shift to System 2 is warranted.
When and why is the more deliberate mode of operation warranted?
A board getting this right is absolutely essential to great governance.

Let me illustrate. Earlier in the book, I related my difficult experience as a director of a failing company. The company had been

growing rapidly by opening new stores and taking on debt to finance growth. Results were good, and the stock price was rising. In my judgment we, the board, were attentive, but we were somewhat lulled by good results just as the self-serving attribution bias would predict, so our monitoring was probably more System 1 than System 2.

For me, things began to change as I tried to make sense of an emerging pattern of events: same store growth slowed, our very capable CEO resigned, I observed sloppy housekeeping in a warehouse tour, and then I encountered a stock-out of a popular product in one of our category killer stores. What cinched my thinking that we were in trouble was a debt offering that earned a junk-bond interest rate.

I found myself alone in my study several evenings in a row, deeply engaged in what Kahneman would call System 2 thinking about the situation: slow and deliberate. I put my thoughts together and went to the chairman and other directors. At the time, I felt I failed to sell my point of view about what was happening and the destructive trajectory we were on. Today I realize more deeply that I failed to persuade my board colleagues to join me in moving from a System 1 to a System 2 approach to monitoring the company: slow down, ask hard questions, consider alternative explanations, and follow facts wherever they might lead. More time would be required of the board, the work would be intense, and conflict with management would was likely. It didn't happen. In retrospect, I think the other directors just wanted things to be okay, so they selectively perceived information to support an optimistic conclusion—an example of motivated reasoning. I was incapable of joining that point of view and, as a result, left the board. As reported previously, the company eventually declared bankruptcy.

Here's the point: a board is a small group charged with responsibility to keep an organization on track, avoid mortal risk, and achieve good results. The board hires management to do this work. Directors monitor and assist management. Most of the time, necessarily, the board trusts and supports management and tracks big picture results. Directors challenge and comment on management recommendations but ultimately accept most of them. It doesn't make sense to put management in charge then relentlessly criticize and deny their recommendations and interpretation of results. But there are moments of truth in the life of every board when directors need to shift from System 1 thinking about company matters to slow and deliberate System 2 thinking. At those moments, directors must supplement their normal trust and acceptance with skepticism, scrutiny, in-depth analysis, and serious challenge. *Great governance requires directors to recognize these moments of truth and make the necessary shift in thinking style and board process.*

Matters requiring this shift may be obvious, such as appointing a new CEO, considering a major investment, or deliberating a strategic move such as a big acquisition or selling the company. But sometimes the cue is not so obvious. As my failing company story illustrates, it may not be singular but a pattern of apparently unrelated developments or experiences that together signal cause for board concern. Skilled sense making on the part of individual directors and the board as a whole is essential. Unstructured time for directors— white space—in board meetings, executive sessions, and over meals is vital to allow them to compare perceptions and verbalize emerging concerns with their colleagues.

Kahneman's fundamental insight, that our minds are capable of System 2 thinking but default most of the time to System 1, leads to other findings that are relevant to boards and directors.

Attribute Substitution. In his 2002 Nobel Prize lecture, *Maps of Bounded Rationality*, Kahneman proposed that many errors and biases arise from attribute substitution—substituting an easier judgment for a more difficult one. Two examples are hiring and investment decisions. Both are important for boards.

Hiring decisions should be based on candidate skills and experience related to the job to be done, but that's difficult to determine. So we sometimes make judgments based on how good a speaker or presenter someone is, how attractive the person is, where he or she went to school, or personal chemistry. These are impressions based on System 1 thinking. They may be relevant to the judgment at hand. However, substituting easy and familiar criteria for harder-to-determine qualities and fit can lead to Type 1 and Type 2 errors (i.e., acting on false positive and false negative signals).

Here is Kahneman on just this situation in *Thinking Fast and Slow*: "The question we face is whether this candidate can succeed. The question we seem to answer is whether she interviews well. Let's not substitute."

Investment decisions should be based on an unbiased assessment of fundamental value and future cash flows, but that's hard and uncertain. So we may base a decision to invest on our feelings about the brand, products, or CEO. Some research suggests that even physical proximity can have a bearing on investment decisions (i.e., we feel more comfortable investing in companies that are geographically proximate to us than those that are more distant). These factors may be relevant to good investment decisions, but when making consequential judgments, we need to guard against System 1 thinking that urges us to substitute simple and convenient criteria for the more difficult and relevant criteria required by System 2 thinking.

And More. *Thinking Fast and Slow* is replete with examples of how our perceptions and mental processes can make the boardroom less than objective and rational.

- *Anchoring*: "The firm we want to acquire sent us their business plan, with the revenue they expect. We shouldn't let that number influence our thinking. Set it aside."

- *Availability Cascades*: "This is an availability cascade: a non-event that is inflated by the media and the public until it fills our TV screens and becomes all anyone is talking about."

- *Representativeness*: "The lawn is well-trimmed, the receptionist looks competent, and the furniture is attractive, but this doesn't mean it's a well-managed company. I hope the board does not go by representativeness."

- *Hindsight*: "He's learning too much from this success story, which is too tidy. He has fallen for a narrative fantasy." "Let's not fall for the outcome bias. This was a stupid decision even though it worked out well."

- *Causes and Statistics*: "We can't assume that they will really learn anything from mere statistics. Let's show them one or two representative individual cases to make our case."

- *Judges v. Formulas*: "Whenever we can replace human judgment by a formula, we should at least consider it."

I have observed all these phenomena in boardrooms. Here is an example of *causes and statistics* from my experience with the board of trustees of the University of Illinois to whom I reported.

When I became president of the university, I found an $800 million backlog of deferred maintenance on our three campuses. It was growing by nearly $100 million per year. I knew if we didn't get on top of the problem, it could reach the point of no return (i.e., certain buildings would be beyond repair and have to be razed). My predecessor and I arranged for many data-based presentations to the board on the deferred maintenance problem but to no avail.

We did not get action until I invited the Dean of the Literature, Arts and Sciences College on the Urbana campus to make a personal report on Lincoln Hall, the cornerstone building of higher education in Illinois, where she had her office and taught courses. Sarah described having to prop open windows with chairs and interrupt her lecture while a squirrel ran across the stage of the auditorium. She showed color slides of Lincoln Hall's terrible disrepair. The board was horrified. This carried the day! We proposed—and the board approved—a program to arrest and whittle down deferred maintenance at U of I. Toward the end of my presidency, the board approved a comprehensive renovation of Lincoln Hall. As Kahneman observes, showing representative cases with stories and pictures can motivate far more learning and action than presenting statistics.

Another concept that is important in business and, therefore, for boards is what Kahneman calls *judges versus formulas*. Simply stated, standardized, formulaic approaches can often produce better results than thousands of individual human decisions. Take, for example, yield-management systems in the airline and hotel businesses that adjust prices in order to maximize revenue through volume (filled airline seats and hotel rooms) times price (per seat or room) depending on supply and demand conditions. It would be naive to think that gate agents and hotel clerks could do as well. The book and movie *Moneyball* is an entertaining portrayal of a statistical versus human (talent scout) approach to player selection in baseball.

Board Process: Brainstorm versus Debate

Insights about board effectiveness can come from unexpected places. A hotly debated *New Yorker* article by a controversial writer, Jonah Lehrer, "Groupthink,"[47] produced a thrill of recognition in me as an experienced director even though it was not about governance.

Lehrer notes the popularity of brainstorming as a technique to improve the creative performance of human groups. He traces the origin of the term and technique to a book titled *Your Creative Power* by Alex Osborn, a partner in the advertising firm of B.B.D.O. in the late 1940s:

> … Osborn's most celebrated idea was the one discussed in Chapter 33, "How to Organize a Squad to Create ideas." When a group works together, he wrote, the members should engage in a "brainstorm" which means "using the brain to storm a creative problem—and doing so in commando fashion, with each stormer attacking the same objective."

Osborn outlined the essential rules of brainstorming including the absence of criticism and negative feedback. As Lehrer reports, "Brainstorming enshrined a no-judgments approach to holding a meeting."

Anyone who has been around the business and education worlds for several decades can attest that brainstorming is something of a religion. Generations of students and corporate employees have been indoctrinated through exercises like the desert (or moon landing) survival problem and the Tinkertoy tower-building competition. Brainstorming is so simple and its benefits deemed so great that even kindergarteners learn it.

Brainstorming begins with a problem for the group to consider. The first and most crucial step is encouraging everyone to offer ideas on how to solve it with no premature evaluation or, especially, critical judgment of any of them, no matter how loony or ill-informed. (Osborn wrote, "Creativity is so delicate a flower that praise tends to make it bloom while discouragement often nips it in the bud.") Once the idea generation stage has run its course, the group uses a democratic process, such as rating or voting on the alternatives, to determine the best course of action. In structured exercises like the desert survival problem, groups learn that the average of individual scores is almost always worse than the group's scores when compared to the best solution of an expert panel.

The gist of Lehrer's article is that these results are impressive but suboptimal. If our goal were to teach people how to attack problems in groups, he says, we would educate them on how to *debate* rather than simply brainstorm.

Lehrer describes a 2003 experiment by Charlan Nemeth, a Berkeley psychology professor, who gave 265 undergraduate students divided into teams of five the same problem: "How can traffic congestion be reduced in the San Francisco Bay Area?" Some teams were given brainstorming direction. Others were told to brainstorm, but with this addition: "...most studies suggest you should debate and even criticize each other's ideas," which they were encouraged to do. The rest of the teams received no instruction and were free to collaborate as they wished. Teams had twenty minutes to come up with as many good solutions as possible. The results:

> The brainstorming groups slightly outperformed the groups given no instructions, but teams given the debate condition were the most creative by far. On average, they generated nearly 20 percent more ideas. After the teams disbanded, another interesting result became apparent. Researchers asked each subject individually if she had any more ideas about traffic. The brainstormers and the people given no guidelines produced an average of three additional ideas; the debaters produced seven.

Another experiment found that people are more creative after hearing an *incorrect* answer to a question. Nemeth observes,

"Authentic dissent can be difficult, but it's always invigorating. It wakes us right up." Dissent, of course, requires dissenters, group members with a genuinely different perspective who are willing to share it.

To illustrate a kind of diversity that can be of real value to work groups, Lehrer recounts a study by Brian Uzzi, a Northwestern University sociologist, of hit Broadway musicals. Uzzi asserts that musicals are a model of group creativity, requiring a composer, lyricist, and librettist as well as director, choreographer, and so on. He wondered whether results were better with a group of strangers or close friends who had worked together before. He found that the relationship between the makeup of the group and the quality of the result was curvilinear, like many in social science. Networks with an *intermediate* level of social intimacy—a measure of the density of connections he called Q—produced the best Broadway shows.

> Uzzi's favorite example of "intermediate Q" is *West Side Story.* ... The concept was dreamed up by Jerome Robbins, Leonard Bernstein and Arthur Laurents. They were all Broadway legends, which makes *West Side Story* look like a show with high Q. But the project also benefitted from a crucial injection of unknown talent, as the established artists realized that they needed a fresh lyrical voice. After an extensive search, they chose a twenty-five year old lyricist who had never worked on a Broadway musical before. His name was Stephen Sondheim.

I noted earlier in the book that diversity of perspectives, experience, career stage, and age is vital for boards to excel. It is for the same reason that Uzzi cites to explain his findings:

> The best Broadway teams, by far, were those with a mix of relationships. ... These teams had some old friends, but they also had newbies. This mixture meant that the artists could interact efficiently—they had a familiar structure to fall back on—but they also managed to incorporate some new ideas. They were comfortable with each other, but they weren't too comfortable.

Similarly, the best boards, in my experience, comprise a core group of directors who know each other well and have worked together effectively for a long time in full collaboration with newer, usually younger board members, who unsettle the status quo and effectively challenge established views and ways of doing things. Over time, the original core group retires, novice directors become the new core of veterans, new directors are recruited and the board is renewed.

Toward Better Board Process

Great governance requires a board to do the right things and to do things right. Substance and process both need to be excellent.

Some aspects of doing things right are straightforward, as reflected in the top-ten lists for directors and boards at the beginning of this chapter. Doing these things won't guarantee quality governance, but they lay a strong foundation.

Doing things right also means ensuring that the boardroom is a place of good information, rational analysis, quality discourse, careful consideration, and wise judgment. Of the three elements that will determine if this is the case, board structure, while always important, is the least potent. Far more consequential are *people*—capable and conscientious directors who are intent on working this way—and a *process* that facilitates it.

There are daunting impediments to boardroom rationality identified by behavioral research. From Simon's bounded rationality to Kahneman's System 1 and System 2 thinking and their consequences, organizational realities and the human thought process can confound even well-intentioned directors in their quest for quality governance. Many boardroom follies are best understood not as the product of evil, negligent, or inept directors and executives but as the result of perfect storms of inadequate or incorrect information, distorted perceptions, biases, and misplaced confidence about judgments that require careful, deliberate System 2 thinking.

When people learn about such follies, it is natural for them to believe that "it would have been different if I'd been there" or "it couldn't happen to me." I'd caution against such hubris.

Boards intent on great governance need to take action to minimize the probability of going off the rails because of organizational and psychological impediments to rationality in the ways they go about their work. It would be nice to think that forewarned is forearmed. Surely a director reading this chapter will come away with better awareness of bounded rationality and the problematic consequences of attribute substitution, anchoring, and the rest in board deliberations and decisions. Presumably knowledge is power, so boards and directors who are informed about these matters should do a better of job of self-monitoring and taking preventive action.

But Kahneman is cautionary. He reminds us that the way we think, especially our fast-thinking System 1, is hard wired and, as a result, difficult to change even with awareness. For example, while I've been more cautious and attentive while driving in novel situations since the accident I described earlier, I know that over time, vigilance fades and System 1 thinking is the default in a routine task like driving. Risk rises.

Kahneman has written recently on executive decisions.[48] He asserts that awareness of cognitive processes that can produce judgment errors does not, in itself, constitute prevention of those errors. He and his coauthors suggest that executives (and presumably boards) use a decision quality-control checklist prior to making major decisions (e.g., pricing changes, capital outlays, and acquisitions). The checklist has a dozen items, including

- Is there any reason to suspect motivated errors or errors driven by the self-interest of the recommending team?
- Have the people making the recommendation fallen in love with it?
- Were there dissenting opinions within the recommending teams?
- Could the diagnosis of the situation be overly influenced by salient analogies?

Separately, four steps are recommended to adopt behavioral strategy to de-bias strategic decisions[49]:

- decide which decisions warrant the effort
- identify the biases most likely to affect critical decisions

- select practices and tools to counter the most relevant biases

- embed practices in formal processes

I understand the checklist and recommendations. But as an experienced director, I can't imagine boards or executives using them mechanistically, and maybe that's the point. In governance and senior management, part of being *seasoned* is having a deep, intuitive understanding of the impediments to rationality in organizational dynamics and individual decision-making. The best, seasoned executives and directors have the habit of questioning, challenging, and guiding others to overcome these impediments, especially when the stakes are high.

Perhaps it's the reason that great leadership, often attributed to an individual, is so often the result of a great *team*: Sam Zell and Bob Lurie of Equity Group Investments, the organization of which the EQR business was originally a part; Paul and John Gordon of Gordon Food Service; Henry Schacht and Jim Henderson and, more recently, Tim Solso and Joe Loughrey of Cummins; Warren Buffett and Charlie Munger of Berkshire Hathaway; Larry Page and Sergey Brian of Google; and, the most unforgettable duo I ever met in the nonprofit sector, the late Father William Cunningham and his parishioner Eleanor Josaitas, co-founders of Focus: HOPE in Detroit. Such partners tend not to be identical but complementary. With a foundation of shared goals and values, but with somewhat different mental habits and biases, I suspect that the partners substantially increase each other's rationality by comparing perceptions and, through discussion and debate, reducing bias.

I know Sam Zell, but regrettably, I never had the opportunity to work with Bob Lurie. People tell me that Sam and Bob were, in some respects, as different as night and day. But together, over thirty years, they made business decisions that created enormous value for their investors. I'll never forget Sam describing his and Bob's mutual trust this way: "We lived out of the same checkbook for thirty years!" I know what a loss it was to Sam, personally and professionally, when Bob tragically died of cancer at age forty-eight. How rare and wonderful is a partner who can improve one's thought processes and the quality of decisions simply by working together day in and day out, year after year, decade after decade?

Obviously, there is no easy way to ensure that a board is *doing things right*, so I offer these practical suggestions:

- Recruit to the board people with a variety of experiences and viewpoints who are willing and able to bring them to bear on vital board decisions.

- Set a goal of making the boardroom a place of good information, rational analysis, quality discourse, careful consideration, and wise judgment. In the board and director evaluation process, assess whether that's the case. Do what's required in terms of tone, leadership, membership, and process to make and keep it that way.

- Combat arrogance and cultivate humility. Overconfidence leads to autopilot (System 1) thinking, which is especially risky in novel situations.

- Consider carefully which matters that come before the board deserve a conscious shift from System 1 (fast) to System 2 (slow, deliberate) thinking. They include big personnel, policy, and investment decisions. But things that are out of the ordinary, such as a requested exception to policy, or any pattern that seems unusual or troubling, should cause a board to slow down and apply System 2 thinking.

- Build plenty of white space in and around board meetings so directors can, in an unpressured way, compare perceptions and try out on each other the sense they are making of what they see, hear, and feel and concerns they have about it.

- Make sure that there is plenty of *debate* in the boardroom. It should be about consequential things. Debate is essential for the board to look at matters from multiple angles, generate new ideas, and come to quality, considered judgments.

Conclusion

Great governance requires directors not only to do the right things but also to do things right. This entails effective work processes by individual directors and the board as a whole. Behavioral research is shedding much light on impediments to rational decision-making and means of combating them. Effective stewardship by the board depends more on good process than good intentions.

A large body of thought has emerged in recent years about what is commonly called *good governance*. We turn next to practices that have real merit and can make boards more effective.

CHAPTER 6

Embrace the Best of "Good Governance"

Emerging Orthodoxy

A book on governance would be incomplete without taking note of the search for good governance practices over the last thirty years. It began with the shareholder rights movement of the 1980s and 1990s and accelerated with federal legislation following the corporate failures and scandals of the last fifteen years. We have seen good governance initiatives on the part of legislators and regulators, reformers, stock exchanges, activist and institutional investors, and proxy advisory services. Corporate boards have been much affected by these initiatives, and much has changed in boardrooms as a result. The initiatives have spilled over into the nonprofit world as nonprofit boards adopt committee structures and board practices, such as regular executive sessions, that mimic those in the corporate world.

As a result, there is today emerging orthodoxy (accepted wisdom) as to what constitutes good governance. In this chapter, I describe and evaluate that orthodoxy then highlight practices that experience and research suggest are most valuable. My advice to boards and directors is to embrace what's best and be skeptical of the rest.

Governance Best Practices Flowing from the Shareholder Rights Movement

The shareholder rights movement ushered in vast changes in public company governance. Three are most important:

- *From* CEO, management, and stakeholder primacy *to* shareholder and board primacy
- *From* boards dominated by chairmen/CEOs and inside directors *to* boards dominated by independent directors representing primarily owners' interests
- *From* executive compensation composed of salary, annual bonus based on performance against plan, and many perquisites *to* compensation composed of salary and short-term bonus with few perquisites plus heavy use of restricted stock and stock options

Good governance practices for public companies spawned by the shareholder rights movement include:

- smaller, more active boards (typically nine to twelve members)
- annual election of directors
- board independence from management (the CEO is usually the only inside director)
- separation of chairman and CEO roles and/or appointment of a lead independent director
- key committees (audit, compensation, governance) composed of independent directors only
- regular meeting attendance (no more directors with membership on a dozen or more boards and predictably spotty attendance)
- regular executive sessions of independent directors

- equity-based compensation (stock and option ownership by management and directors)
- required director skills, especially financial literacy

I watched these changes play out in boardrooms. They led to a new tone of urgency and seriousness about shareholder value. They stimulated a newfound willingness to jettison CEOs of underperforming companies along with more demanding performance standards. Boards increased their focus on earnings and total shareholder return. They reinforced the focus with equity-based compensation.

Did the changes matter? I think so. In the twenty years from 1960 to 1980, major stock market indices grew hardly at all. In the thirty years between 1983 and 2013, concurrent with the shareholder rights movement, they have soared, increasing by a factor of ten despite two major market meltdowns. While the bull market has had many causes (low interest rates, a technology explosion), it would be hard to argue that the shareholder rights movement, with its focus on earnings and the governance and compensation changes it triggered, didn't contribute to these results.

Changes in public company governance spilled over into the board practices of many private companies and nonprofits. For example, I observed in both settings creation of audit, compensation, and governance committees and increased frequency of executive sessions.

By 2000, most boards subscribed to good governance orthodoxy. Then came the biggest wave of corporate scandals and implosions in decades. High-profile companies collapsed between 2000 and 2002, including Enron, Adelphia, Tyco, and WorldCom. So did the gold standard audit firm, Arthur Andersen, after being found guilty of criminal charges related to Enron.[50]

There was much public consternation about governance failures at these companies. While it is unclear whether the new governance orthodoxy contributed to the failures (e.g., by inadvertently incenting excessive risk taking with massive stock option grants), it clearly did not prevent them.

One governance scholar observed at the time that examination of boards of the failed companies left one puzzled as to the board's culpability.

> [There was] no broad pattern of incompetence or corruption. In fact, the boards followed most of the accepted standards for board operations: members showed up for meetings; they had lots of personal money invested in the company; audit committees, compensation committees and codes of ethics were in place; the boards weren't too small, too big, too old, or too young. While some boards had problems with director independence, this was not true of all failed boards and board makeup was generally the same for companies with failed boards and those with well-managed ones.[51]

Into this quandary waded legislators and regulators, determined to improve board accountability and performance.

Government's Efforts to Fix Failed Corporate Governance

The years 2002–2010 were a consequential period for corporate governance legislation. First came the Sarbanes-Oxley Act of 2002 and eight years later the Dodd-Frank Act of 2010. Governance reforms were included in these laws because corporate fraud and failure inevitably led to questions: Where were the directors? Why didn't boards prevent the failures and scandals? Both laws have had a material effect on boardroom practices and the environment in which governance operates.

Sarbanes-Oxley

President Bush signed the Public Company Accounting Reform and Protection Act (as it was called in the Senate) and Corporate and Auditing Accountability and Responsibility Act (the House of Representatives name) on July 29, 2002. Sarbanes-Oxley, named for the Democratic Senator and Republic Congressman who sponsored the bill, was a direct response to the corporate scandals and failures of the previous two years in which both boards and audit firms were deemed to have failed investors, employees, and the public. The financial shenanigans and unreliable financial statements of Enron, WorldCom, and Tyco, certified with clean opinions by their auditors, made legislative response inevitable.

Five (about half) of the provisions of Sarbanes-Oxley (SOX) relate to governance:

- *Corporate and Criminal Fraud Accountability.* Criminal penalties are established for manipulation, destruction, or alteration of financial records or other interference with investigations. Whistleblowers are protected.

- *Corporate responsibility.* Senior executives take individual responsibility for the accuracy and completeness of corporate financial reports. Principal officers—usually the CEO and CFO—personally certify and approve the integrity of company financial reports quarterly.

- *Enhanced financial disclosures.* Effective internal controls are required to ensure the accuracy of financial reports. Timely reporting is required of material changes in financial conditions and stock transactions of corporate officers.

- *Audit independence.* Conflicts of interest are limited (e.g., restrictions on providing non-audit services), and audit partner rotation is required.

- *PCAOB (Public Company Accounting Oversight Board).* An entity to conduct independent oversight of public accounting firms is created.

These provisions are consequential for public company governance. Arguably most important is the effect on audit committees.

Since 1972, when the SEC first recommended that public companies establish audit committees, their importance in corporate governance has grown. In 1987, the Treadway Commission made recommendations aimed at deterring fraudulent financial reporting. In 1999, the Blue Ribbon Committee made recommendations to improve audit committee effectiveness that resulted in changes in listing standards by the New York Stock Exchange and NASDAQ.

The main functions of the audit committee are to oversee the financial reporting process, monitor the choice of accounting policies and principles, monitor the internal control process, oversee the hiring and performance of the external auditor, and ensure open communication among management, the internal and external auditors, and the audit committee.[52]

SOX affected audit committee requirements in three areas: composition and authority, external audit, and internal control. Specifically, the Act requires that all members of the committee be independent and have the authority to engage special counsel or experts to advise them with funding provided by the company. The Act specifies that the committee must preapprove audit and non-audit services by the external auditor; receive reports directly from the external auditor on critical accounting policies, review material communications with management, and other matters; and ensure the quality of internal control, including procedures to receive and handle internal complaints and protect whistleblowers.

SOX delivered an unmistakable message: with the assistance of the external and internal auditors and any other advisors and experts required, audit committees are to oversee and ensure quality financial reporting and internal control processes that underpin it.

Dodd-Frank

President Obama signed the Dodd-Frank Wall Street Reform and Consumer Protection Act of 2010 into law on July 21, 2010.

Dodd-Frank was the legislative response to the 2008 financial crisis, regarded as the worst since the Crash of 1929. The crisis included the collapse of large financial institutions like Lehman Brothers and AIG, bursting of the U.S. housing bubble, federal bailouts for multiple companies (including General Motors and Chrysler), and a bear market that cut the value of major stock indices approximately in half before rebounding. At the center of the financial crisis were excessive leverage and risk taking by financial institutions and individuals. Accordingly, the Dodd-Frank Act focuses on the institutional framework for financial regulation, establishing, for example, the federal Financial Stability Oversight Council and the Office of Financial Research and expanding the regulation of hedge funds and the insurance industry.

Dodd-Frank affects corporate governance through Subtitles E (Accountability and Executive Compensation) and G (Strengthening Corporate Governance) of Title IX of the Act (Investor Protections and Improvements to the Regulation of Securities).

Enacted in an environment of public outrage about the role of executives of some financial firms and perceived failure of their boards, Dodd-Frank has a strong emphasis on executive compensation. Executives of these firms made enormous amounts of money in the years leading up to the crisis because of activities that later proved toxic. Many people (including me) believe that the *design* of executive compensation plans encouraged excessive risk taking and outsized rewards for what proved to be bad bets with disastrous consequences for companies and the country.

Accordingly, Dodd-Frank requires that the compensation committee of the board be comprised only of independent directors, that the board provide more complete disclosures about executive compensation in the Compensation Discussion and Analysis (CD&A) section of the annual proxy statement, and that SOX's rules regarding clawbacks of executive compensation be expanded.

The Act creates a *say-on-pay* mandate requiring periodic shareholder advisory votes on executive compensation. It affirms that the SEC has authority to promulgate proxy access rules allowing shareholders under certain conditions to use the company's proxy statement to nominate candidates to the board. Both provisions fulfill long-held aspirations of good governance advocates.

The Act requires that companies disclose whether the same person holds both the CEO and chairman of the board positions and why. This provision reflects a growing belief that the combined role vests too much authority in one individual and weakens the oversight role of the board. It partially fulfills another aspiration of governance reformers.

Accountability and Executive Compensation. At least once every three years, a public company is required to submit to a shareholder vote approval of executive compensation (say on pay).[53] Shareholders are provided the ability to express disapproval of any golden parachute compensation to executives through a nonbinding vote. They must be informed of the relationship between executive compensation paid and the financial performance of the company. The company must report on the median of the annual total compensation of all employees and the chief executive officer's compensation, including the ratio between the two. All members of the compensation committee of the board must be independent directors. The company must report on incentive compensation with commentary on whether it could lead to material financial loss to the company and whether the compensation is excessive.

Strengthening Corporate Governance. The SEC is permitted to issue rules and regulations that enable a shareholder to use a company's proxy solicitation materials for the purpose of nominating individuals to membership on the board of directors. Previously, investors who wanted to replace directors had to bear the cost of mailing separate ballots and waging a campaign.

The SEC issued a new regulation providing for proxy access in August 2010. In July 2011, a federal appeals court threw out the regulations on grounds that the SEC did not adequately analyze the costs to U.S. companies of fighting in contested elections. It also said the agency failed to back up its claim the rule would improve shareholder value and board performance.[54] In the aftermath of this ruling, some shareholders are putting forth proxy access proposals of two types to companies: precatory and binding. Precatory proposals ask the board to take such action as may be necessary to allow proxy access, such as amending the bylaws, while binding proposals directly amend the company's bylaws.[55]

Dodd-Frank is clearly intended to increase board attentiveness to executive compensation practices, especially as they affect unwise risk-taking by senior executives and lead to excessive compensation based on short-term results. It also represents a win for certain governance reforms.

Good Governance Templates and Report Cards

Today, there are many corporate governance *templates*, sets of practices asserted to compose the elements of good governance. Institutional investors like TIAA-CREF and CalPERS propagate them to communicate their governance expectations to companies in which they invest and to guide their proxy voting. Others are used by ratings agencies such as S&P, Moody's, and Fitch as part of their process for assessing company financial risk. Large, international audit firms do work in governance as a service to their clients. Some unions and religious orders are active in governance. They tend to have special interests reflecting the values of their members and the priorities of their organizations.

These organizations produce a tremendous amount of descriptive and explanatory material about their criteria and methods for evaluating corporate governance. Much is publicly available. An informed consumer of this information will recognize a good deal of overlap in assertions about what constitutes good governance. The templates of TIAA-CREF and CalPERS are representative.

TIAA-CREF

TIAA-CREF manages over $500 billion in investment assets on behalf of 3.9 million individual clients. In its statement on Corporate Governance for Portfolio Companies, TIAA-CREF says that its "views on corporate governance are founded on our conviction that good corporate governance should maintain the appropriate balance between the rights of shareholders—the owners of the corporations—and the needs of the board and management to direct and manage effectively the corporation's affairs." In its Summary of Proxy Voting Policies, TIAA-CREF says,

> The Funds seek to use proxy voting as a tool to promote positive returns for long-term shareholders. We believe that companies that follow good corporate governance practices ... are more likely to produce better returns than those companies that do not.

TIAA-CREF makes explicit its views about good governance and the basis for its proxy voting practices through a twenty-page, published policy statement on corporate governance comprising five sections:

- TIAA-CREF's Corporate Governance Program
- Shareholder Rights and Responsibilities
- Corporate Governance Principles
- Environmental and Social Issues
- Proxy Voting Guidelines

Among the policies:

- TIAA-CREF urges fair treatment of all shareholders by companies in ways both financial and nonfinancial (e.g., clear communication and robust disclosure).

- The organization emphasizes the responsibility of shareholders as providers of capital to pay attention (hold the board accountable, monitor performance) and be constructively active (e.g., promote aligned compensation and demand the integrity of accounting statements).

- TIAA-CREF expects the board to represent the long-term interests of shareholders by overseeing strategy development and implementation, assuring financial integrity, developing compensation and succession planning policies, setting the ethical tone, and holding management accountable.

- Most directors should be independent, and all should be elected annually with a majority of votes cast. A director in an uncontested election who does not win a majority should submit his or her resignation to the board, which should promptly decide the matter and disclose its rationale. Shareholders should have legal and reasonable proxy access.

- With regard to board duties, directors should monitor and oversee management in areas of vital interest to shareholders, directly and through its key committees (compensation, audit, nominating and governance); participate in developing the strategic plan; select and evaluate the CEO and plan succession; and develop an equity policy that determines the proportion of the company's stock to be made available for compensation, including clear limits on the number of shares to be used for option and other equity grants.

- The board should be neither too large (for collegial discussion) nor too small (to ensure the requisite expertise). Executive sessions and board self-evaluation are expected. The chairman and CEO roles should be separated, or a lead independent director should be appointed.

- Board committees are to have charters and the power to hire independent advisors. They are to report to the full board. Each shareholder initiative is to be reviewed by the relevant committee as is the proposed management response.

- Executive compensation is to be carefully and thoughtfully designed to fit the circumstances of the company. It should be linked to metrics that drive long-term sustainable value. Factors to consider include a mix of cash and equity, a logical performance measurement cycle, and incenting performance but not excessive risk. Compensation should be "reasonable by prevailing industry standards" and "fair relative to pay practices throughout the company." Caution is counseled with regard to compensation consultants, pay comparisons, and a proper mix of the formulaic and judgmental in performance evaluations and the terms of employment contracts.

- TIAA-CREF offers extensive guidelines for equity-based compensation and the Compensation Discussion and Analysis section of the proxy.

- TIAA-CREF identifies environmental and social issues with which it expects boards to be concerned. These include environment and health, human rights, diversity and nondiscrimination, philanthropy, corporate political influence, and product responsibility.

- TIAA-CREF describes its policies on a long list of proxy voting issues. These range from director elections and auditor ratification to animal welfare and predatory lending. In every area, the organization states its policy, indicating *will generally support, will generally not support, or will consider on a case-by-case basis.*

CalPERS

CalPERS is the California Public Employees Retirement System, which manages investments that pay for retirement and health benefits for 1.7 million beneficiaries. In mid-2013 it had over $250 billion in assets under management. On its Global Governance (subtitle: Investing with a Sustainable Framework) website, CalPERS states that, "We believe good governance leads to better performance. We seek corporate reform to protect our investments. The global governance team challenges companies and the status quo."

Since the mid-1980s, CalPERS has been a pioneer in corporate governance activism. CalPERS's statement on *Global Principles of Accountable Corporate Governance* addresses the question "What have we learned over the years?"

> We have learned that (a) company managers want to perform well, in both an absolute sense and compared to their peers; (b) company managers want to adopt long-term strategies and visions but often do not feel their shareholders are patient enough; and (c) all companies— whether governed under a structure of full accountability or not— will inevitably experience both ascents and descents along the path of profitability.

> We have also learned and firmly embrace the belief that good corporate governance—that is accountable corporate governance— means the difference between wallowing for long periods in the depths of the performance cycle and responding quickly to correct the corporate course.

CalPERS's principles of accountable corporate governance guide its proxy voting and "provide a foundation for supporting the System's corporate engagement and governance initiatives to achieve long-term sustainable risk adjusted investment returns."

The document uses the term *shareowner* versus *shareholder* throughout "to reflect a view that equity ownership carries with it active responsibilities and is not merely passively 'holding' shares."

CalPERS's Global Principles are organized into four areas: Core, Domestic, International, and Emerging Markets Principles.

Core (i.e., universal) principles cover

- *Optimizing shareowner return*—governance should focus on optimizing the company's operating performance, profitability, and return to shareowners

- *Accountability*—directors to shareowners and management to directors

- *Transparency*—operating, financial, and governance information readily transparent

- *One-share/One-vote*—all investors treated equitably

- *Proxy Materials*—written in a manner to enable shareowners to make informed voting decisions

- *Code of Best Practice*—to be issued by each capital market to promote transparency, avoidance of harmful labor practices, investor protection, and corporate social responsibility

- *Long-term Vision*—directors and management to have a vision that emphasizes sustained shareowner value

- *Access to Director Nominations*—by shareowners

CalPERS's Domestic Principles of Accountable Governance apply to U.S. companies. They embrace the Council of Institutional Investors Corporate Governance Policies and cover seven areas. There is much overlap with TIAA-CREF's proxy voting policies. Principles include:

- *Board Independence and Leadership.* Majority of independent directors, executive sessions, independent board chairs except in limited, explained circumstances, lead director otherwise, retiring CEO not to sit on board (definitely not on committees), independent committees.

- *Board, Director and CEO Evaluation.* Board talent assessment and diversity (broadly defined), expectations and annual evaluation of board, committees and directors, CEO performance criteria and regular evaluation, CEO and director succession plans.

- *Executive and Director Compensation.* For executive compensation, structure and components designed by board and disclosed to shareholders; mix of cash and equity including base salary and short- and long-term incentives linked to performance resulting in shareowner value creation; guidelines on timing and nature of performance metrics and hurdles; clawback policy; extensive guidance (dos and don'ts) on use of equity in compensation; severance agreements and retirement plans. For director compensation, cash and stock with equity ownership requirement.

- *Integrity of Financial Reporting.* Integrated reporting of financial, environmental, social, and governance performance; desirability of convergence to global accounting standards; guidelines on external auditor, audit committee, and audit disclosures.

- *Risk Oversight.* Policies, procedures, reporting, and decision-making to manage, evaluate and mitigate risk; be a "risk intelligent" company.

- *Corporate Responsibility.* Policies regarding human rights violations, environmental disclosure, sustainable corporate development, reincorporation and charitable and political contributions.

- *Shareholder Rights.* Majority voting, special meetings and written consent by shareowners, shareowner resolutions, no greenmail, poison pill approval by shareowners, annual election of directors, cumulative voting right in contested election of directors.

TIAA-CREF, CalPERS, and other institutional investors place high priority on shareholder value and a proper balance of authority between shareholders and boards and boards and management. They value incentive compensation and conservative compensation practices. Broader concerns including sustainability and corporate social responsibility are more recent entries.

Governance Ratings

Public companies are rated on their corporate governance practices by a handful of influential companies, including GMI Ratings, Glass Lewis & Co., and ISS. A younger director recently asked me, "How should I think about the governance ratings?"

I answered with an analogy. There is a lot of similarity between governance ratings and the business school and university ratings and rankings of which I am a veteran as a former b-school dean and university president. In both cases, I have been guided by the same principles:

1. Pay attention to them—they matter. Ratings affect perceptions of quality and can improve performance.

2. Make your goals substantive: quality governance with excellent results for companies, academic excellence for universities. When you succeed, you'll do well enough in the ratings and rankings.

3. Think independently. Some of what constitutes best practice today will have enduring value, but some will be revised over time. Decide what applies to your situation and act on it.

GMI Ratings

GMI Ratings is "an independent provider of research and ratings on environmental, social and governance and accounting-related risks affecting the performance of public companies."[56] GMI Ratings was formed in 2010 through the merger of three firms: The Corporate Library, formed in 1999, which was a pioneer in corporate governance ratings; Governance Metrics International, founded in 2000, which developed in-depth coverage of governance risk profiles of 4,200 U.S. and international companies; and Audit Integrity, founded in 2002, which developed accounting and governance risk (AGR) ratings for 18,000 public companies worldwide.

GMI calls its evaluations of companies ESG (environmental, social, and governance) ratings. It generates ESG ratings for more than 6,000 companies worldwide as well as AGR ratings for approximately 18,000 companies. GMI asserts that its ESG ratings "help investors assess the sustainable investment value of corporations."

"The ESG Ratings model is based on a carefully crafted list of over 100 ESG KeyMetrics, organized into six individual scoring components"[57]:

- Environmental key metrics produce an environmental rating

- Social key metrics produce a social rating

- Board, pay, and ownership and control key metrics produce, respectively, a board rating, pay rating, and ownership and control rating. These three ratings produce a governance rating.

- The environmental, social, and governance ratings produce an ESG rating for the company

All metrics are derived from publicly available information about the company. "As of February 2012 there are 120 key metrics used to score each company, but fewer than half of those account for nearly 90% of the total possible scoring for all components." Governance-related metrics account for 72 of the 120 Key Metrics used for scoring.

For each key metric, GMI Ratings uses pass/fail evaluation. Each failed metric is indicated in the GMI analyst research platform by a red or yellow flag to indicate the degree of impact on the company's rating. Individual company scores are assigned on the basis of these key metric flags, as weighted then converted to percentile ranks from 1 (worst) to 100 (best). ESG ratings are expressed as letter grades:

Percentile	ESG Rating
96–100	A (Superior)
76–95	B (Above Average)
26–75	C (Average)
6–25	D (Below Average)
1–5	F (Failing)

GMI Rankings makes qualified but strong assertions about the value of its ratings for investors, stating, "ESG data and analytics can be valuable tools for both the long and short side of an investment strategy." Examples cited include:

- "BP's 2010 Deepwater Horizon explosion and oil spill came after GMI Ratings had warned of the company's negligence in safety and environmental issues."

- "Pre-hacking scandal, GMI Ratings rated News Corp poorly for the Murdochs' disproportionate influence on the board and related party transactions with the family."

- "GMI Ratings identified weak boards at Lehman Brothers, AIG, Countrywide and General Motors before the 2008 financial crisis."

These are intriguing assertions, but for anyone trained in research methods, they invite a question about the frequency of false positives in GMI's ratings (i.e., the number of times a weak rating is *not* followed by a significant corporate problem).

Glass, Lewis & Co.

GL is an indirect, wholly owned subsidiary of Ontario Teachers' Pension Fund board. Glass Lewis and ISS are the dominant proxy advisory services to institutional investors.

In its 2013 proxy paper on EQR, GL lists all proxy voting issues then notes, without comment, the board's recommendation and GL's. The paper provides descriptive information about the company and a comparison of EQR and several competitor/peer companies on key financial measures. A section follows on each proxy voting issue. For EQR in 2013, there were four: Election of Trustees, Ratification of Auditor, Advisory Vote on Executive Compensation, and Shareholder Proposal Regarding Sustainability Report. GL concurred with the board's recommendations on all four issues.

On trustee elections, GL compares the NYSE and NASDAQ listing standards on director independence, committees, executive sessions, and so on and notes that GL has stricter standards for favorable proxy voting recommendations. EQR meets these higher standards, which contributed to Glass Lewis's favorable recommendation on trustee elections.

GL examined the fees EQR paid Ernst & Young for audit (90 percent of total fees) versus non-audit services (10 percent), concluded they were reasonable, and recommended ratification of E&Y's appointment.

GL did extensive analysis of EQR's executive compensation and provided substantial commentary about what they liked (alignment of pay with performance) and didn't like (the structure of the incentive compensation program—too discretionary in their view). They recommended a favorable vote.

The fourth voting item in 2013 was a shareholder proposal from the Office of the Comptroller of the City of New York. It represented a number of public employee pension funds and requested that the board "prepare and make available to shareholders by September 2013 a sustainability report" addressing the company's efforts involving energy, water, waste, and other environmental impacts. The board recommended against it on the grounds that the company was committed to sustainability, had appropriate policies and practices in place, and provided sufficient public disclosure. GL concurred.

ISS

ISS, originally Institutional Shareholder Services, has been owned by three companies over the last seven years. When corporate directors think of governance evaluation, ratings, and rankings, they usually think of ISS because of its pioneering role in the field. The ISS methodology for evaluating a company's governance practices that was introduced in 2013 is called QuickScore. It replaced the Governance Risk Indicators (GRId) method that was in place for three years. QuickScore ranks companies in deciles within each of ISS's four pillars—Audit, Board Structure, Compensation, and Shareholder Rights—and provides an overall governance rating.

What does an ISS governance scorecard look like? I annually review ISS's report to institutional investors on EQR's governance along with their recommendations on proxy voting.

ISS's 2013 report on EQR begins with a table recommending favorable votes for all of EQR's eleven trustees, ratification of Ernst and Young as the company's auditor, a favorable advisory vote on Named Executive Officers' Compensation and a favorable vote on a shareholder resolution that would have required the company to produce a sustainability report. These recommendations concurred with the board of trustees' recommendations with the exception of the final item.

The report then presents a Financial Highlights section including a comparison of EQR's financial performance (Total Shareholder Return or TSR) over 1-, 3-, and 5-year periods of 2.4 percent, 22.46 percent, and 13.90 percent, compared with the GICS 4040[58] TSR of 20.37 percent, 15.00 percent, and 4.86 percent and the S&P 500 TSR of 16.00 percent, 10.87 percent, and 1.66 percent over the same periods.

This section also includes a five-year history of EQR's stock price compared to an index of real estate investment trusts and the S&P as well as five years of financial and operating performance on measures like profit margin, return on equity and assets, price earnings ratio, and TSR in comparison with five other real estate companies selected by ISS.

The report provides a detailed and informative report on EQR's Corporate Governance Profile. The section includes a Board and Committee Summary including these topics:

Trustee independence	82% are
Separate chair and CEO	yes
Lead independent trustee	yes
Voting standard	majority
Resignation policy	yes
Number of trustee-owned shares	15,043,000 / 3.3% of shares
Percentage of trustees with stock	100
Attendance <75%	none
Trustees on excessive # of boards	none
Average age	59
Average tenure	10 years
% of women on board	18

Details are provided on each trustee's independence, affiliations, employment, board compensation, and EQR equity ownership.

The report presents a compensation profile offering an executive pay overview, option valuation assumptions, CEO pay multiples, CEO pay details, and dilution and burn rate under the company's equity compensation programs.

Next in the report is the company's ISS QuickScore in the four pillars noted above: Board, Compensation, Shareholder Rights, and Audit. Each pillar comprises three to seven subcategories that may be green-starred (indicating a subcategory has been awarded the highest number of points) or red-flagged (indicating points at the bottom of the range). What follows is the longest section of the report: recommendations on each of the 2013 proxy voting items with supporting analysis. Some sections are extensive, notably the Executive Compensation Analysis, which among other things examines pay related to performance and CEO pay magnitude.

Over the years, I have found ISS's descriptive and analytical work informative and useful. I have at times disagreed with their GRId and QuickScore ratings of EQR, finding them formulaic versus considered. Fortunately, ISS's voting recommendations often appear to reflect considerations beyond what the ratings alone might indicate.

Evaluating Good Governance

Practices that make up good governance orthodoxy have emerged over the last thirty years from the shareholder value movement, federal legislation, and governance ratings. To what extent do they contribute to great governance? *Corporate Governance Matters*, a book I use in my graduate governance course and to which I referred in the previous chapter, reviews research on the relationship between governance practices and corporate financial performance.

Shareholder-Friendly Practices

Corporate Governance Matters (CGM) begins with an examination of the relationship between *shareholder friendly* practices and *corporate performance*:

> As we will see throughout this book, many studies link measures of corporate governance with firm operating and stock price performance. Perhaps the most widely cited study was done by Gompers, Ishii, and Metrick.[59] They found that companies that employ "shareholder-friendly" governance features significantly outperform companies that employ "shareholder[-]unfriendly" governance features.[60]

Gompers, Ishii, and Metrick used 24 governance rules to construct a governance index as a proxy for the level of shareholder rights at about 1,500 large firms during the 1990s. They found that an investment strategy that bought firms in the lowest decile of the index (strongest rights) and sold firms in the highest decile (weakest rights) would have earned abnormal returns of 8.5 percent per year between 1990 and 1999. They found that firms with stronger shareholder rights had higher firm value, higher profits, higher sales growth, lower capital expenditures, and made fewer corporate acquisitions.

These are eye-opening findings for shareholders and boards. Using a continuum between the extremes of "tilts toward [shareholder] democracy" to "tilts toward [management] dictatorship," the authors conclude that governance practices that favor management (including board) entrenchment are related to lower corporate performance and shareholder value. They divide these *shareholder-unfriendly* practices into five groups:

- *Delay*—tactics for delaying hostile bidders (e.g., classified board)

- *Voting*—voting rights (e.g., unequal shareholder voting rights or supermajority requirements to approve a sale or merger)

- *Protection*—director/officer protection (e.g., golden parachutes)

- *Other*—various takeover defenses (e.g., poison pills)

- *State*—state laws (e.g., business combination law, fair price law)

Most of the twenty-five variables across these five categories are anti-takeover measures, that is, they make it more difficult to acquire the company.

The authors find that boards and management that are more insulated from the market for corporate control oversee companies with inferior financial performance and shareholder returns compared to boards and managements that are less insulated. The difference in excess returns to shareholders of more *democratic* versus *dictatorship* portfolios was significant: 23.3 percent versus 14.1 percent between 1990 and 1999.

Good science requires the ability to replicate studies and generate similar findings. Given the importance of the Gompers, Ishii, and Metrick study, there have been a number of efforts to confirm their findings. At least one study[61] appears to, but several do not. While it is intuitively appealing that a lower level of anti-takeover practices will result in better returns to shareholders, and some studies support this conclusion, not all do. Larcker and Tayan conclude, "Currently, researchers have not produced a reliable litmus test that measures overall governance quality."[62]

Nonetheless, the shareholder rights movement resulted in most boards dismantling most takeover protections. This makes sense. Boards represent shareholders. If in doubt, the tilt should be toward them. Today the burden of proof is clearly on the board and management as to why a particular practice that might reduce the company's exposure to the market for corporate control is in the best interest of shareholders.

Board Structure and Composition

Much good governance orthodoxy focuses on board attributes that are structural and easily measured. In my experience, directors are often skeptical about whether these attributes really affect corporate performance in a robustly positive way.

Is separating the chairman and CEO roles better than a combined chairman and CEO? Does having a lead independent director make a difference? What about more outside, independent directors? Does the presence on a board of particular kinds of professionals (e.g., financial experts) matter? Do company policies restricting the number of boards on which a director can serve make sense? What about board size: are smaller boards better than larger? What about diversity of directors?

CGM reviews research on the relationship between these attributes of boards and company performance and concludes, "A casual reading of this information indicates that very modest evidence supports the adoption of many of these attributes."[63]

I would emphasize *very modest* at least as much as *supports*. Also, the type of research on which the findings are based is not capable of establishing with certainty a *causal* relationship between the variables studied and corporate performance, further weakening the very modest evidence that supports adoption of these attributes.

CGM summarizes research findings on the relationship between board structure and corporate financial performance in the following table:

Summary of [Corporate] Performance Effect for Selected Board Structural Characteristics[64]

Board Structure Attribute	Findings from Research
Independent chairman	No evidence
Lead independent director	Modest evidence
Number of outside directors	Mixed evidence
Independent directors	No evidence
Independence of committees	Evidence for audit committees primarily
Representation of:	
Bankers	Negative evidence
Financial experts	Positive for accounting professionals only
Politically connected directors	No evidence
Employees	Modest evidence
Busy boards	Negative evidence
Interlocked boards	Evidence for performance, against monitoring
Board size	Evidence for small boards (in simple companies) and larger boards (in complex companies)
Diversity	Mixed evidence
Female directors	Mixed evidence

In other words:

- There is no evidence that having an independent chairman (versus combined chairman and CEO) is related to better corporate performance.

- There is modest evidence that having a lead independent director is related to better corporate performance.

- Having directors who serve on too many boards (*busy boards*) is related to worse corporate performance.

- Most variables have a mixed or ambiguous relationship with corporate performance.

Given the highly equivocal research findings about these governance attributes, following are some lessons from experience—my own and that of other veteran directors with whom I have conferred—about attributes I deem most important.

Independent Chairman v. Chairman and CEO. This choice is highly situational and person-dependent for a board. Reformers who favor a universal requirement for independent chairmen view it as an always-desirable antidote to the problem of imperial CEOs. For example, David Nadler, in a thoughtful commentary on the subject, concludes,

> Today, given the evolution of governance in this country and in the interest of sustaining governance of the highest quality, I recommend that boards formally designate a nonexecutive chairman. In my opinion, other things being equal, the nonexecutive chair should be regarded as the superior structure because it provides more clarity of board leadership and offers more advantages.[65]

This is overkill. A board should be able to choose whether to separate or combine the roles, depending on the company's leadership needs and the people involved.

For example, I have no doubt that Equity Residential is well served by Sam Zell serving as chairman, as he has for twenty years, with another executive—currently David Neithercut—serving as CEO. Zell is a visionary in real estate. Part of his value to EQR is the broad overview and network of relationships he develops through involvement in multiple companies, deals, and financing arrangements. Zell's focus is the world and EQR's place in it. Neithercut's is on the management of EQR's business—its properties and residents, strategy, people, operations, and financing. Zell and Neithercut are highly complementary and have the great chemistry required for an effective partnership between chairman and CEO.

By contrast, it is clear to me that in some situations, a single leader serving as chairman and CEO is more effective.

As described earlier, in 1999 Tim Solso became chairman and CEO of Cummins, Inc. At the time, Cummins was soon in the throes of recession after two decades of relentless change and improvement but struggling profitability.

The story of Cummins' survival through the recession, followed by a decade of growth and profitability, is extraordinary.[66] In crisis, Cummins needed strong, unambiguous leadership. Its tradition was to have a single chairman and CEO. Tim Solso made big bets and, with a leadership team led by his long-time colleague and great operating executive, Joe Loughrey, executed them brilliantly. I have no doubt that the situation required a chairman and CEO, and fortunately for Cummins, Solso was right for the job. It would have been regrettable for the Cummins board to have to contort the leadership arrangement with a separate chairman to meet a universal standard of structure at the most senior level.

Lead Independent Director and Executive Sessions. I served on boards for many years when the concept of a lead independent director did not exist. Creation of this role has been a very positive development. On two boards where I serve, we have both a non-CEO chairman *and* a lead independent director. It's that valuable.

The lead director chairs executive sessions of the independent directors. Executive sessions used to be rare and nearly always signaled crisis. Now they are standard practice and extremely valuable. The lead director works with the chairman and CEO or chairman/CEO to ensure that matters of concern to independent directors are on the agenda. The lead director is a focal point for both independent directors and management who can confer with him or her on any matter of concern. I give the development of lead directors as well as frequent executive sessions an A+ in contributing to good governance.

Independent Directors, Committees, Busy Boards, and Board Size. Public company boards now, by and large, comprise exclusively independent directors with just one insider: the CEO. Overall, this is a good thing. Shareholders have a clear set of interests, and executives *can* have incompatible interests like high compensation unrelated to performance. Even though some non-independent directors in the past provided very valuable service (e.g., members of law firms and investment banks who knew the company well), their conflict of interest was problematic.

Independent directors compose the full membership of public company audit committees and, in most cases, compensation and governance committees. This is a good because it is in the work of these committees that the interests of shareholders—not management—must be paramount. *CGM*'s report that there is a positive relationship between financial experts on the board and corporate performance should be no surprise. Financial expertise on at least the audit committee is absolutely essential to effective monitoring of financial statements and the system of internal control on which their quality depends.

Research confirms that directors should not serve on too many boards. It's a matter of *attention*. In electing directors, shareholders are buying a share of each director's time, focus, experience, and judgment. It would be very difficult for the CEO of a major company, which is a 24/7/365 job, to be a director of more than one or two companies beside her own. Calendar conflicts alone will create attendance problems, and attendance is the cornerstone of attention.

Board size is an important matter. I served on a large public company board with fifteen members at one time and on another with six. The former was too large for full involvement of all directors. The latter was too small for a proper range of experience and opinions and to get committee work done well. In my experience, this piece of governance orthodoxy—that boards should have from nine to twelve directors—is right. Even here, though, flexibility is essential. For example, a board may temporarily expand in size to bring on new directors in anticipation of the departure of long-serving members of the board, much like having two runners in a lane during the baton pass of a relay race.

Board Diversity. *CGM* reports that ethnic and gender diversity—that is, the presence of minority and women directors on boards—has a mixed relationship with corporate performance. Some studies show a positive effect. For example, Credit Suisse Research Institute reported that shares of companies with a market capitalization of more than $10 billion and with women board members outperformed comparable businesses with all-male boards by 26 percent worldwide over a period of six years.[67] A study by Catalyst[68] came to similar conclusions. However, *CGM* observes that "the study did not include control variables, so it likely omits important explanatory factors, such as industry, company size, or capital structure. More rigorous studies find no relationship between female board representation and performance."

Most corporate boards today are largely made up of white, male directors. Women and minorities make up about 15 percent and 7 percent, respectively, of large company boards. In a forward-looking company, diversity has value for two reasons. One is talent. Women and minorities have been coming up fast in the American workplace and are now better represented than ever, including at the most senior level. The same is true of international employees in global companies. Boards need to put out a *Welcome!* sign to these cohorts as both employees and directors.

The other reason is fairness. Board service is a privilege and responsibility. A fraction of the population shouldn't have a corner on privilege or be disproportionately saddled with responsibility. America works best when doors are open and selection is based on merit. We can look back and appreciate absurdities like private university medical schools admitting few if any Jews. Some of the love of the University of Michigan and University of Illinois I found among Jewish alumni is because these great public universities welcomed them when top privates didn't. The same is true of the color barrier in baseball, *de facto* quotas on African-Americans in the NBA in the 1950s, and so on. Boards should reflect the impressive educational and professional achievements of women and minorities. This is a development in which no board should want to be last.

Audit Committee Practices

Substantial evidence from academic studies suggests that management has the ability and, at times, willingness to manipulate reported financial results. *CGM* cites a study by Burgstahler and Dichev[69] which found that

> [c]ompanies are much less likely to report a small decrease in earnings than a small increase in earnings, even though statistically the distribution between the two should be equal. This suggests that management might manipulate or overstate results to meet targets. Other studies support this conclusion.[70]

Management lives in a pressurized environment of stretch earnings targets and financial incentives to achieve them. A diligent audit committee of independent directors with one or more financial experts is essential. In partnership with the independent and internal auditors, the committee ensures that management's use of discretion in accounting estimates and judgments does not impair the accuracy of financial statements.

Executive Compensation Practices

The board is responsible for determining how and how much to pay executives. It is one of the big things for the board to get right. If total compensation is too high, shareholders' resources are wasted. If too low, the company will not be able to attract and retain needed leadership talent. If the compensation mix is wrong, executives' incentives are distorted and performance can suffer. An important question, therefore, is whether there is evidence of a connection between the quality of governance and executive pay practices and results.

There is, in fact, some evidence that stronger governance results in more conservative executive compensation while weaker governance results in excessive compensation.

One study investigated the relationship between corporate governance and CEO pay levels and the extent to which the higher pay found in firms using compensation consultants is related to governance differences.[71] Weaker versus stronger governance was found to explain much of the higher pay in clients of compensation consultants. The authors measured governance strength versus weakness in over two thousand public companies with eight variables. Five were assumed to relate negatively to stronger governance:

- Number of directors on the board

- Percentage of inside directors

- Percentage of directors sixty-nine years of age or older

- Percentage of directors who are busy (i.e., serve on at least two boards)

- Percentage of outside directors appointed since the current CEO's term began

In other words, a larger number of directors and higher percentages of directors in the other four categories indicate weaker governance. By contrast, a smaller number of directors and lower percentages of directors in these categories signify stronger governance, as does a sixth variable: the presence of an outside chairman. Two additional variables from the company's charter are also included as indicators of governance strength: annual versus staggered director elections and a single versus dual class of shares.

Another study came to a similar conclusion: weak governance systems are correlated with excessive compensation.[72] The authors found an inverse relationship between the quality of oversight that a board provides and the level of compensation within the firm. In this case,

> Companies with weak board oversight are defined as those with dual chairman/CEO, boards with a larger number of "gray" directors (directors who are not executives of the company but who have other financial connections to the company or management as a result of serving as a lawyer, banker, consultant, or other provider of services), boards on which a large percentage of outside directors are appointed

by the CEO, boards with a large percentage of old directors, and boards with a large percentage of busy directors.[73]

These findings square with my experience. A strong compensation committee of truly independent directors and a strong board in total are essential to making executive compensation competitive but not excessive and ensuring that pay is tied closely to performance.

How Good *Is* Good Governance?

In my experience, there are five good governance practices that are clearly valuable and should be embraced by public company directors:

- a strong board comprising primarily independent directors with the time and commitment to be attentive and diligent
- shareholder-friendly policies that reduce board entrenchment
- appointment of an independent lead director and regular executive sessions of independent directors
- a strong audit committee of independent directors to ensure quality financial reporting
- compensation designed by a committee of independent directors that ties pay to company financial performance and total shareholder return over a sustained period

Other practices, like board size and whether to combine or separate the chairman and CEO positions, are best left to the discretion of the board.

Directors know that a "check the boxes" mentality does not guarantee great governance. They question formulaic methods of evaluating and rating governance and seem to understand intuitively what careful scholars like Larcker and Tayan conclude:

[R]esearchers have not produced a reliable litmus test that measures overall governance quality ...[74] and we have seen that most structural features of the board have little or no relation to governance quality.

We have seen that more auditor restrictions have no impact on financial statement quality, that commercial and academic governance ratings systems largely lack predictive ability, and that regulatory requirements for many mandated governance practices have neutral or negative impacts on corporate outcomes and shareholder value.[75]

The implications are clear. Directors should embrace practices such as the five above that are, in my experience, demonstrably valuable. They are entitled to skepticism of strongly asserted but unsupported claims about good governance practices. Perhaps they would be wise to follow the lead of Myron Steele, Chief Justice of the Delaware Supreme Court, who said,

> Until I personally see empirical data that supports in a particular business sector, or for a particular corporation, that separating the chairman and CEO, majority voting, elimination of staggered boards, proxy access with limits, holding periods, and percentage of shares— until something demonstrates that one or more of those will effectively alter the quality of corporate governance in a given situation, then it's difficult to say that all, much less each, of these proposed changes are truly reform. Reform implies to me something better than you have now. Prove it, establish it, and then it may well be accepted by all of us.[76]

Conclusion

Some good governance practices should be embraced while others remain under scrutiny. Still, public company governance in America is better today than in the past for three reasons.

First, boards are far more attentive to shareholder value. This is as it should be. Shareholders are the legal owners, risk takers, and residual claimants of the company after everyone else is paid. They elect the board and rightly expect directors to represent their interests to management while being attentive to related matters as reflected in the Pyramid of Purpose in Chapter 1.

Second, old-style CEO dominance is rare. Most boards today have a healthy and actively engaged relationship with the CEO. Most directors are independent and have been recruited and selected by an independent governance committee. Executive sessions of the independent directors have changed the balance of power with the CEO.

Third, boards and their governance practices are in a fishbowl. While I don't agree with every metric used by proxy advisory services and others who evaluate governance, the evaluation process has value. In the same way that student evaluations make for more attentive teachers, evaluation of governance contributes to directors' attention to their duties and care in their decisions.

The lessons of experience count in governance. In the next chapter, experienced board chairs, CEOs, and directors offer their thoughts on great governance.

CHAPTER 7

Other Voices

Interviews with Board Chairs, CEOs and Experienced Directors

To this point, I have shared with you my thoughts on governance. Now I want to report what I learned from interviews I conducted with experienced board chairs, CEOs, and directors of public and private companies, all of whom also serve on nonprofit boards. Because these are people I know personally, I was confident they would be candid. Because I respect them professionally, I knew their views would be worth hearing.

Equity Residential (EQR) and Gordon Food Service (GFS) figure prominently in my board experience and in this book. Therefore, I report first on interviews with trustees and directors of these two companies, the former public, the latter private.

EQR Trustees on Governance

I interviewed

- Sam Zell, chairman

- David Neithercut, president and chief executive officer

- Chuck Atwood, lead trustee

Sam Zell, chairman

You've said that EQR is one of the best boards on which you've served. Why?

The board takes responsibility. I have thrown out the rope. People either make a lasso or hang themselves. What you have at EQR are people who are really interested. They are there because they have a significant connection to the company. Strong ownership. Generally long tenure.

My policy is very clear: great encouragement for everyone to participate. And they do.

What is your philosophy of governance as board chairman?

It starts with the fact that I value everybody else's time as much as my own. So the board focuses on exercising governance responsibilities, not regurgitation of information that has been presented to them. I assume everyone reads. If there are questions, terrific.

Our meetings revolve around a set of important questions we are trying to answer and senior people to highlight particular areas.

What is the board's job?

To oversee the operation and management of the company and maintain broad perspectives. Not day-to-day involvement but very involved in overall strategy. The board's responsibility is to receive strategy, question and challenge it, accept it and oversee implementation.

You have run big private enterprises. Does a public company board add value?

Having more people at the table expands the possibility of learning more. However, there is a lot of baggage—rules and regulations and evaluators—in the public company arena. Compare it to hotel rating systems. If you study them, you find that if you provide a hair dryer, lotion, etc. (check the boxes), you may be able to qualify as four-star even though the property is really three-star. That's what board evaluations can be like. The public company domain is becoming more and more difficult. You must have people devoted to compliance that you wouldn't consider in a private company. At the same time, access to capital is extremely valuable, but the price has gone up materially for public companies.

What makes for an excellent director?

It starts with absorption of the material. It's very obvious at board meetings who has and hasn't prepared. You must be prepared. Unprepared directors waste other people's time. They ask questions already answered or that don't make any sense.

Second is taking a real interest in management. Directors can be good but not great because they don't create and nurture a relationship with management. Doing so improves your understanding of risk/reward relationships.

Third is being an apolitical director. We had a director once who joined the board and started creating factions—churning up the troops. As chairman, I called him on it. Lobbying and individual advocacy are very deleterious.

There are different kinds of directors. Jim Harper [a founding trustee of EQR, now retired] was a terrific trustee. He was a strategist for lack of a better word. Jim was not so interested in little thinking. Because of his broad perspective, he was a major contributor to the board. That's one kind of director. Another focuses on operational matters, details. There is a role for both. The chairman's role is to maintain a proper balance.

What constitutes great governance for a company?

I think great governance starts with recognition of the stakeholders. The board sets standards of ethics and performance that apply to the whole company. Ethics is not a list but, rather, creating and perpetuating an ethical environment.

Great governance is much more focused on forty-eight months from now than next week. Boards can't do much about next week. Boards can do great things for four to five years from now. Recognize what is within the realm of the possible and focus on the distant tomorrow. In EQR's case, think about going from garden apartments

[EQR's original portfolio] to high barrier-to-entry cities [the current portfolio]. That didn't happen overnight. It took years. We started with Boston and learned we could do it and the advantages.

Great governance means the approach to compensation is right. Incentives matter. The board needs to do it and own it versus companies where compensation is significantly between the compensation consultant and CEO.

What are common director weaknesses?

iPhones in the laps. It's a sign of inattention. Lack of focus. It doesn't happen much in our meetings because of the way they are run. Also, failure to interface with management, be prepared, be "in the room."

What do you think of board reforms of the last decade?

It's interference with the operations of boards and companies. More box checking than true reforms. We could ultimately end up with more professional board members (like politicians—they used to have jobs and businesses) who are less engaged in the company.

What would be your advice to legislators, regulators, and institutional investors who want better governance?

Increase the ownership stake of directors and managers. Not through stock options but through real ownership—and lots of it. Decision makers at risk. There is no other thesis.

What are danger signals that you watch for on the board?

Politicization, faction development. Also, situations develop that require change. Sometimes a director has to leave—unprepared, inattentive, becomes antagonistic. I'm all in favor of people speaking up, but you need a group that has assembled for the purpose of working on behalf of the company, not playing gotcha, etc.

What advice do you have for young directors?

First, don't sit on the board unless you truly understand the business. Learn it. Spend time in the company and with senior people. How do they make money? Understand the customers and what they want.

Second, find ways to interface with management. Have lunch or a drink. Not just the CEO. Over three or four years, find a way to interface with the top six or eight people in the company.

Third, listen. Listening is one of the most important skills in the world and not widely enough practiced. A good board member listens carefully to everything going on, which leads to better understanding.

David Neithercut, president and CEO

What is your philosophy of governance?

Over years of experience, you establish a compass or internal sense and you know what is and is not the right thing to do. That's what guides you. That's my philosophy.

What do you expect of the board?

We need to make sure we have the right strategy and people and are executing well.

So I look for the board to challenge my thought process and arrive at the right decision, then support us. I worry about groupthink. We always ask: what would the other guy say about this? The board needs to check, test, challenge, prod—then join arms and go forward. This is the single most important thing to me as CEO—especially on strategy.

Also, boundaries are important. Boards direct and govern, management manages. Within these boundaries, challenge and support by the board are most important to me as CEO.

What is the purpose of the board?

To represent the shareholders. Plain and simple. Shareholders vote directors in, so that's their responsibility.

Could you cite examples of high value contributions by individual directors?

In Archstone [a major acquisition by EQR in partnership with Avalon-Bay in 2012], Sam [Zell] was terrific. On this enormous transaction, he repeatedly outlined the risks he saw and his concern about them. He didn't just will it to happen. Rather, he offered honest risk assessment and invited a lot of discussion. This helped me a lot—not because I hadn't thought of these things but rather because of the sounding board and blessing it provided. Sam strongly supported Chuck's two-step process [Chuck Atwood, lead director, recommended a multi-day pause for questions and consideration between presentation of the transaction to the board and board approval]. He understood and accommodated what the board needed to do on this transaction.

Chuck has really been helpful to me about process. I mean the process needed to get the board to consider a transaction and approve it or not. How to bring the board along, involve them, get their input and, ultimately, approval. I hate to use this term but it is vital to manage the board well. This does not mean manipulation.

My attitude is that we're all in this together. I'm not the imperial CEO. I have a lot of smart people on the senior team and on the board and my goal is that we all join arms. Bringing along the board is important. I have to make sure my team and I communicate frequently with the board. I've learned the importance of it because of the radio silence I've experienced as a director elsewhere. Communicating frequently is key to bringing the board along.

What constitutes great governance?

Doing the right thing. This is like my philosophy of governance. There is a right way to do things. There is no road map. When you encounter things, you just know they have to be dealt with and how.

In a situation in which a large but not controlling stake has board representation, I feel a great responsibility to ensure all shareholders' interests are represented. Over time, with experience, you develop a compass that tells you how things need to be done. And you do it. Example: a right versus aggressive way on a transaction might take an extra ten days, $50,000 legal fee, etc. Chuck's process was the right way to bring the board along in this transaction [Archstone]. A lot of it has to do with directors being truly independent, treating them and doing things that way. Make sure they're informed, take the time, provide expertise, enable them to exercise independent judgment.

What makes for an excellent director?

You can tell who is engaged and who's not. The interest they show, the work they do outside the boardroom. Getting to know the company.

An excellent director knows how to maneuver in the boardroom. The boardroom has a culture. Successful people can navigate it. A coach told me once that too many people just dive straight into problems. You need to dance with problems. Jim Harper [a founding trustee of EQR] knew how to do it. Jim used to identify problems one or two board meetings in advance. He'd say to me, "One of these meetings, we ought to talk about *x*," rather than putting Sam in a corner or embarrassing me.

No showboating. If you have a problem, call the chairman or me. That's dancing with the problem.

It's good to have sitting CEOs on a board for the perspective they bring. But we need grinders, too, to get all the work done. It's impossible to be a fully engaged CEO and a grinder on a board other than your own.

Weaknesses you've seen in directors?

Weaker directors bounce on the surface. They know enough to check a box or say something. They are into best practices, box checking. They sit on other boards, hear buzzwords, throw them out there, etc.

What are danger signals you watch for?

I watch for dysfunction. The board not being able to conduct its work. Meeting but not fulfilling its responsibilities. Going through the motions versus thoroughly and thoughtfully conducting the business of the board.

Advice to new directors?

You have a lot to learn and it's very hard to learn it in a few hours each quarter. Develop relationships with executives outside the boardroom. It will make you more effective in the boardroom. Learn how to get things done.

What do you think of board reforms?

I think, overall, really good. I was not a board member back in the day—maybe others see more negative impact. My experience started in 2000.

I think director and committee independence is terrific—get away from the friends of the CEO. A separate chairman and CEO is the right way to go. I am surprised how many companies keep them linked. A lead trustee is not the same thing.

Board size. I prefer not to have it any bigger than nine to twelve; it's tougher to manage. Be careful not to have too many committees. That could require more directors—not a good thing.

Executive sessions are so important. How could there ever have been a time when there were none?

Compensation. Will anyone ever be happy with compensation? No. More disclosure hasn't helped much.

Sarbanes-Oxley and Dodd-Frank. Something was needed. But there have been a lot of unintended consequences because a few companies screwed up. The price corporate America has paid for Enron, WorldCom, etc. has been huge.

Advice to legislators, regulators, etc. who want better governance?

It's hard to legislate or regulate these things well. I'm concerned about getting good people to serve, especially on audit committees of big, complex companies. Many people decline to serve on audit committees.

Chuck Atwood, lead director

What is your philosophy of governance?

By governance, I mean the process by which board does its work and carries out its duties.

My philosophy is that directors direct and management manages. Governance sets the rules under which those things take place. The issue is always how the intersections of these roles is handled. A director of a company in which I was an executive once said to me, "Don't make me manage; you won't want me to."

The duty of the board is to owners, not others. Management has duties other than just to the owners. It's important for the board to understand why management does what it does and why there might be a difference of opinion with management.

If directors don't like the way something is being managed, the solution is to change the manager, not try to manage it themselves.

What do you expect of the board?

I expect the board to perform its duties on behalf of the owners.

A clear example was Harrah's [Chuck was vice chairman and CFO]. The company was sold to private equity. It's clear in retrospect that was good for the owners. We harvested a lot of value. The board ensured that the transaction would close and capture the maximum value for owners. There was a potential for conflict of interest with management as we would receive not only the equity payoff, we would also stay with the company and could have conflicting interests. So the board ensured the purchase price was proper for all owners.

The board ensured the deal was fair, the process was solid, and the transaction would close. The board spent a lot of time on each of these resulting in a deal that was in the best interest of all owners.

What do you think constitutes great governance?

Great governance takes place when everybody on the board understands his or her role and does the job expected. It's vital for directors to understand why they are on the board, what is expected of them as a result, and then deliver it. Directors are selected because they are expected to add something to the board's ability to do its job. It's important each understands what that is then delivers it. Example: Mary Kay Haben on the EQR board [former senior executive of Kraft and Wrigley]. She understands CEO perspective, operations, marketing, branding. She brings that knowledge and experience to the board.

What makes for an excellent director?

Excellent directors are committed and passionate about creation of value for the owners. That includes a willingness to work. Being on the board is not just an honor. It comes with a responsibility to work. Prepare for meetings and offer business judgments and experience. Help the group dynamic of the board.

What are weaknesses you see in directors?

Failure to do the above things. Sometimes directors just don't contribute. The opposite can be a problem, too: directors grandstanding on certain issues, becoming obsessed about them, can't move on to the work of the board. They need to be reminded that their obsessions are not the only things for the board to consider.

Danger signals in governance dynamics?

I look for certain signals like complacency, lack of continual learning, and lack of respect for the roles of management and the board.

Advice for new directors?

New directors should understand what their duties are. Understand why they are on the board and what the board wants from them and what they want out of board service. Listen to what other experienced directors are doing and saying, how they interact. Learn from that.

What do you think of governance reforms?

I would say governance reforms, on the whole, have been generally good. A lot of the reforms have involved checking boxes to be sure things are done. There's nothing wrong with that if you understand the reasons for completing the work to check the box. The overall result: better boards, more dedicated board members. The days of seeing a directorship as an honor only are gone, but there has been some punishing the innocent for the sins of a few. That's why compliance alone is not enough—you need to understand why the activities are required.

The best things that have happened: greater independence including the concept of "trust but verify," greater clarity of roles of board and management.

Net effect of Sarbanes-Oxley and Dodd-Frank?

While in both cases a lot of punishing the innocent, the result has generally been positive. Section 404 [of Sarbanes-Oxley, on internal controls] was a pain, but it caused us to put a lot of focus on better controls. It focused our attention on doing what we said we were doing so it could be easily audited.

The jury is still out on Dodd-Frank. In my view, trying to solve compensation through rule making is probably not effective. So far, it has called a lot of focus and attention to compensation, but I haven't seen any evidence it has changed anything.

Advice to parties who want better governance?

I would urge them to focus on education of boards and directors on their duties and roles. Put less focus on rule making. Reformers should be very hesitant about broadening the duty of boards, for example from enhancing value for owners to ensuring employment. That would set up conflicts that boards can't manage effectively.

GFS Directors on Governance

I interviewed:

- Dan Gordon, chairman
- Jim Gordon, president and CEO
- Dave Gray, independent director

Dan Gordon, chairman

What is your philosophy of governance?

The overarching mission of the board is to ensure the health and vitality of this company in perpetuity. That's a compelling aspiration for us. That's what we are trying to accomplish. It captures what we are trying to do on a big picture basis.

Our philosophy emanates from Paul and John [Dan's father and uncle, founders of the company in its modern form]: a small board with a high level of commitment and engagement and a deep understanding of the business.

Did you have a board before 1987 [when the current board was created and outside directors brought in]?

It was just the officers. We looked at financial results. We met quarterly. Had dinner together on Monday night, came back to the office by 7:30 pm, worked until midnight. We went through a level of detail that wore you out. Driving through numbers. I asked Dad why we didn't meet in the morning. "No," he said, "those are working hours!"

When Paul and John decided in 1987 to pass the generational baton to us and consider retirement, I think they believed that when I became CEO, I would need help. So they created a real board and brought in Dave and you. They did it as much for me as anybody.

What contributions do you try to make as a chairman?

I try to balance demanding high performance and communicating that expectation each year with encouraging management, empathizing with them enough to say, "Look, we have a lot of challenges, we know you're out there doing your best." Stretch and support. It's a fine balance. It's hard to achieve. I think management appreciates the board meetings. They come away challenged and refreshed.

As chairman, what's most important to me is that we move forward with one voice—providing clear direction to management. It requires a lot of mutual respect, camaraderie, and chemistry. When things get out of sync or there are misunderstandings, the role of chairman is to sniff things out and figure out what to do about them.

I expect us to achieve consensus as much as possible. Stay at it until we can. We don't vote very often.

What do you think constitutes great governance?

You don't know if you're achieving it until you look back and have the benefit of time. Our first task was to set things up in governance that would last. To take something that Paul and John and others before them built over decades, then move it to the next generation and next level. For Paul and John to watch over it while letting go—

that's great governance. Now we get to do it all over again for the next generation.

What did we create? A small board of advisors and a board of directors. Family control even if there is no family in the business. The assignment you and Dave got was to set up governance arrangements that will last a hundred years and more. We got off to a great start by looking ahead three or four generations and creating arrangements, separating control from management, if necessary. Then we had twenty years to get it going with Paul and John watching. I think that's been great governance.

What makes for an excellent director?

Discernment and wisdom. Big picture thinking to craft a future—envision it. Having a very good understanding of leadership and people. Time and commitment are really important. Many board members could be so much more helpful if they took the time to be engaged. Connecting to the core values of a business and a family—that alignment is everything in a private company. Discernment—being able to read between the lines, an intuitive sense of things, seeing below the surface, understanding an issue beyond its face value.

What are danger signals you watch for in governance?

When there is not obvious consensus. Tension that doesn't get resolved. Also complacency—just accepting management's view on things. People not really being into it as evidenced by attendance and tardiness problems, checking their phones during meetings. Not capturing their interest and attention and excitement.

What advice would you offer to directors who are new to board service?

Every director wants to contribute. But the first way you contribute is to shut up, listen, and learn. Don't feel you have to impress people by speaking. Tracy [one of GFS's newer directors] observed and listened, handled the process of just fitting in. We expect you to apply yourself by learning the business. A fraction of what you need to learn is at the meeting. It's the preparation and one-off dinner with a member of management and a follow-up conversation—that's where value is. We have a long view of your value as a director.

What would be your counsel to a senior executive with a board opportunity?

Why are you interested? What intrigues you about the company? What makes it a compelling consideration? What do you know about the people with whom you'll be working? Do you admire and respect them? Do you have the time required—because it will be more than they tell you. How are you going to add value?

What do you think is unique about serving as a director of a private, family-controlled company versus a public company?

Positive: The informality we have. Much less baggage due to lower compliance requirements. Board members can get involved in many areas of the business. The board is where the action is versus committees with larger boards.

Negative: You have to deal with the family. Dealing with family is not always a picnic.

Why do you choose to have a board at GFS? It's optional for a private company.

Having had a board, I can't imagine not having it in terms of the support and accountability it generates, the exposure it gives us to many different environments that board members operate in. It has made all the difference here. It's vital to have non-family board members both for the business and the family. We would not have accomplished anything like what we have without the board and outside directors.

A public company gets access to public capital markets but there's a lot of baggage. Private companies don't get that access but there is much less baggage.

Here's something powerful. Paul gave you guys [the two outside members of the board of advisors] the keys to the place. There are five votes on the board of advisors that controls the company and two went to outsiders. This engenders a tremendous sense of responsibility. Most private companies have advisers to whom they listen if they want to and ignore if they don't. That's not true here.

Jim Gordon, CEO

What is your philosophy of governance?

I grew up in the business while being on the board of directors. I have learned so much through observation of our board and also through nonprofit board involvement.

What's important to me is a lack of politics and personal agendas. Everyone needs to be on the same page, wanting what's best for the organization.

Most of the time, the board should be a gentle guiding force that directs and advises management, every now and then pulling back on the reins. The board shouldn't lean too far forward into tactics and operations. Let management handle it. I see this a lot on nonprofit boards—directors who want to run things.

A good board needs to ask good questions. Provide guidance this way versus giving orders.

What do you as CEO expect of the board?

Clear direction on big issues and strategic plans. Say, "I'm concerned," and raise questions when that's the case. Help management sort out a good strategic plan, then let them run with it.

Have the wisdom to say, "That's a little out of bounds, that's getting away from core values and competencies." Specific strengths of directors: financial, legal, people. Both Dan and I without you guys [the independent directors] would be in a world of hurt. I marvel at Paul and John finding you guys and what you have brought in parallel but different ways through your skill sets and encouragement.

Policies the board has developed on key issues like debt and employment of family members in the business are very helpful to me as CEO and to the family.

What is great governance?

I can point to a lot of things. Like our decision to go to Canada, then expand into western Canada. The board was right there, ready to approve. Sorting through difficult senior management situations. Helping solve tough problems.

What makes for an excellent director?

A broad skill set across the portfolio of directors. Bringing insight from outside the company.

The motivation—believing in what the organization is doing, passion for our mission and what we stand for. Really caring.

Being able to ask the right questions at the right time versus showing off with a question. Sincere people who fit the mission and culture.

What are danger signals you watch for?

Extremes—directors who are too involved or not involved enough. The goal is a golden mean: caring and being passionate but not getting into management.

What is your advice for new directors?

Listen. But don't be bashful about asking questions. Learn how to bring up issues and ask questions in a way that is not off-putting. The key is a sincere desire to understand. Wonder more than tell. It's an art. You know it when you see it and when you don't.

Why do you choose to have a board as a private company?

The outside perspective, especially in a family business, is crucial. We behave better as a family with non-family directors present. It brings professionalism to how we run the business (e.g., financial reporting). Having a board and outside directors pushes us that way.

I have told family business councils to whom I've spoken: if you don't have a board with outsiders, you need to. It has raised our game so much. For example, the outside directors pushed for audited financial statements. I gulped at the expense. But we needed to do it. We have created disciplines that are as good as public companies and they have enabled us to grow and expand.

Dave Gray, independent director

What is your philosophy of governance?

The purpose of the board is to enhance shareholder value. Here, we also perpetuate and protect the culture of the company and foster a growth environment. Everything we do comes back to those two things and their connection to shareholder value.

The board must focus on senior leadership. Who's going to be in charge?

We must be sure to have the right governance structure and people and then perform well as a board. This requires constant monitoring.

With regard to business strategies, the board must be far enough in to know they are valid and executable and reflect the right balance of risk and reward. We set growth and value expectations for management on behalf of shareholders.

Directors get involved in a detailed way selectively on issues, drawing on their networks and experience. We do so without getting into management and operations. For example, a director made a connection for management to the private equity owner of restaurant chain. A phone call opens up a door.

What are the main contributions you try to make as a director?

Coaching is a big part of it. Drawing on twenty-five years of experience that goes back to having worked with the current day founders and carrying forth that knowledge to the current generation of managers. Also, I can bring in lessons from business in general that I have been involved in.

More personal for me was laying the foundation for the company's planning process. It took really well, and I am pleased to see how good management is at it now. Before, they were mainly doers; now they are planners, too.

Staying close enough to people in business to sense the tone of things. Char [Dave's wife] and I have been on many award trips, and we have interacted with thousands of GFS people. It helps me understand the state of our health. This is more doable for a director in a private company. It follows the example set by the Gordons in terms of staying close to the people.

Getting involved in the "big bet" decisions. Management has a lot of latitude to make decisions, so I need to be close enough to know when a big bet is being made and insert myself to evaluate, decide, help close the deal.

What is great governance?

The key thing for the board is our decision-making process. Make decisions quickly but on sound, fact-based information. Create discipline and insist on this information.

Because of our size and informality and ability to gain quick consensus, our decision process is fast. This creates competitive advantage and helps management. For example, an acquisition target we were pursuing in western Canada: the board was in a lunch meeting, we had to make a $10 million decision in the negotiations. It was recommended and we decided on the spot. We need to work to keep this capability as the company gets larger and more complex.

Achieving results and minimizing risks along the way. Minimizing reputational risk. Being sensitive to the consequences of our decisions and actions for our reputation.

Accessibility to the board by management. You were asked to present to customers of the Great Lakes East division. No management would have done this at Sara Lee [where Dave worked for a time] with board members. People are comfortable to bring sensitive issues to the board; they don't feel they are putting themselves at risk.

How do we get through leadership succession at all levels? Note how seamless the Paul Gordon succession was when he passed away. This is how it should be for all positions. We need to lay a foundation for it.

What makes for an excellent director?

A good listener more than talker. A measured risk taker. Understand the business. A servant leader.

Weaknesses in directors?

Inadequate time commitment, not making it a priority. Not being a balanced risk taker. Too conservative. Poor relations with the CEO. Not taking time to understand the industry and business.

Danger signals you watch for on the board?

A willingness to accept too much or too little risk. Making decisions about risk without good information. Poor instincts about risk—

reckless or too conservative. Decisions that put the entire company at risk can be fatal.

Disregard or lack of respect for the governance process—short-cuts, violating disciplines.

When there is an absence of consensus, the matter should not be left unresolved.

Poor attendance, not making it a priority. Think of your and my attendance record at GFS—we have not missed more than one meeting in twenty-five years.

What advice do you have for new directors?

Study the business, understand our competitive position, how we go to market, what our value propositions are. Understand risk/reward; don't join the board if you're excessively risk averse.

Examine the reasons you are joining the board. Is it for stature and your bio or genuine interest in the business and the owners? In a private company, understand what the business means to the owners.

Initially listen and absorb, maybe for a couple of years. Then transition into asking the right questions

Understand the priorities of the shareholders. At GFS, it is enhancing value but also balancing resources between the business and the charitable work that is the family's main focus. You need to understand this to do a good job for the owners.

Don't join the board without a long-term commitment. This results in your taking a long view of things. It takes time to add value.

What is the difference in serving on the board of a private versus public company?

There are two types of private companies: family versus investor owned and controlled.

In a family company, there can be a lack of outside pressure for performance. So the origin of high performance standards is the board.

There is usually a longer time horizon for decision-making in a family company.

Protecting the reputations of both the business and family is vital.

There are fewer financial disclosure requirements for private companies—not just revenue by line of business but margins, cost structure, financial strength.

In a public company, you work for nameless, faceless shareholders. In a family company you know the owners on a first-name basis. Decisions you make affect shareholders you know.

You make tradeoff decisions in a private company between keeping resources in the business and paying out to shareholders. Dividend and other payout policies are not so much financially driven as personal. Desire for liquidity can create a lot of conflict and destroy businesses and families.

Public companies have an advantage in their access to capital. It's a problem to be solved in private companies.

As an outside director, never consider yourself family in a family business. You don't necessarily have a right to the same benefits, authority, and privileges as family members. You need to remain very objective.

A Virtual Conversation with Board Chairs, CEOs, and Directors

I had the opportunity to interview individually some extraordinary men and women on their views about governance. In this section, I create a virtual conversation among them by posing questions and sharing their responses. These individuals have served on both public and private company boards, as noted, and numerous nonprofit organizations. Those interviewed include

- Linda Walker Bynoe, trustee of EQR, director of Anixter International, Northern Trust Corporation and Prudential Retail Mutual Funds (public)

- Dave Downey, director of M Financial Holdings and M Life Insurance Company (private), First Busey Corporation (public), Champaign-Urbana IL News-Gazette, Inc. (private)

- Errol Halperin, partner, DLA Piper, former trustee of EQR, director of multiple public and private companies

- Bill Hall, former chairman and CEO, Falcon Building Products (public), acquired by private equity in 2000; director of W.W. Grainger, Actuant, and Stericycle (public)

- Rick Hill, former chairman and CEO, Novellus Systems, Inc. (public), acquired by Lam Research for $3.3 billion in 2012; director of Arrow Electronics, LSI, Cabot Microelectronics, Tessera, and Planar Systems (public)

- Mannie Jackson, chairman, Boxcar Holdings (private); former owner and chairman, Harlem Globetrotters (private); director, Acorn Energy (public), Epic Research & Diagnostics, and Arizona Diamondbacks (private) and former director of multiple public companies including Ashland Oil, Jostens, Reebok, Stanley Black & Decker, Transamerca, and True North

- Peter Mullin, cofounder and chairman, M Financial Holdings (private); founder, Mullin Automotive Museum (nonprofit); director, Avery Dennison (public)

- Don Parfet, director, Kelly Services, Masco, and Rockwell Automation (public) and numerous private companies

- Tom Siebel, founder and former chairman and CEO of Siebel Systems (public), acquired by Oracle in 2005 for $5.8 billion; chairman of First Virtual Group and C3 Energy (private)

- Tim Solso, former chairman and CEO, Cummins, Inc. (public); chairman, General Motors (public); director, Ball (public).

What is your philosophy or set of guiding ideas about governance?

Solso: Directors are the stewards of the company and need to take a long-term perspective. The board must ensure the company is making responsible decisions, considering the interests of all stakeholders including customers, employees, suppliers, shareholders, community, etc.

There is often no one right answer and the board has to consider the complexities of an issue and either recommend or make a decision based on the facts, what is right and appropriate.

Also very importantly, the board needs to assess the quality of the leadership, including their character and values and the systems and process for the ongoing development of leaders.

Hill: Corporate governance revolves around making sure the board is focused on the best interests of the shareholders at all times—over the short-, mid-, and long-term and making tradeoffs among these three.

You want directors who understand the difference between the role of the board and the role of operating management. The board gives input and its best advice. Management makes decisions real time, taking this advice into account along with other information. If management consistently makes wrong decisions, the board needs to change out the CEO. The board advises and counsels management.

Mullin: Recognize that the traits that built an entrepreneurial company, like singular focus and running over or through all barriers, are often opposite of what is required to maintain a large, successful one, such as shared responsibility, glory and equity, allowing others to shine, considering all factors in promoting excellence.

Jackson: Directors are like firemen. They can sit around the firehouse and play cards, but their work comes in crises. When they are a good team, know the company well, work well together, then they can perform in crises, of which there are many.

Murphy: I start with shareholders first—stakeholders in nonprofits. I also believe that objectivity and independence in all things are vital. We have to avoid conflicts and manage those that exist.

We need to be knowledgeable about the business—really understand what will make the business successful. Stay focused on the long term and don't get caught up in quarterly results. We have to monitor them because of trends but not overreact, no knee jerks.

Halperin: Recognize the trust and confidence shareholders have placed in you. You are a fiduciary: assume fidelity responsibility to avoid fraud, waste, and embezzlement. Identify risks to the company and mitigate them. Ensure the highest ethical standards at the board and management levels. Recruit and select the best possible top management, evaluate their performance, act accordingly. Understand the company and its industry.

Hall: The board works for the shareholders, not the Street, etc. We are fiduciaries for people like you and me. We represent them.

Downey: The purpose of the board is to hire the CEO. Then you are a sounding board and learning place for the CEO in representing the views of ownership—because you represent them.

Parfet: The board's most important job is hiring and developing the CEO. Finding individuals with the requisite skills to be CEO is usually quite easy. Supporting the development of a CEO in order to lead a high-performance team to outperform in the marketplace can be quite demanding.

Bynoe: Similar to my philosophy in business, it is always about the people. They make the difference. Bring the best people to the table in the boardroom and management. Share a common set of core values—integrity, ethical behavior, transparency, fairness, respect. That is the beginning and the end of great governance.

What do you expect of the board and individual directors?

Siebel: My expectation is that the board is engaged and well prepared, asks challenging questions, and is available to assist outside scheduled board meetings.

I want directors to be committed to the success of the company, not just going through the motions. I put together spectacular boards at Siebel Systems and C3 Energy—Chuck Schwab, George Shaheen, Eric Schmidt, etc. They set a tenor for the quality of communication.

No one wants to look bad in front of these guys. Their very presence takes your game to a level you've never played before.

Solso: I want directors to be totally aligned with the values and strategy of the company. I have seen directors who are willing to cut corners. I have heard directors say during breaks, "Well, I don't really buy the strategy." Yet they remain silent during the meeting. Directors need to be engaged and enthusiastic. They must have good attendance and come to meetings prepared and well informed. It's not acceptable for directors to sleep, do their e-mail, or be preoccupied with something other than the business at hand. It sends the wrong signal, especially to management attending meetings.

Mullin: Be prepared in advance. This seems obvious but you wouldn't believe how many directors are scrambling to read material before they walk into the board meeting. Be willing to challenge management. The desire to be collegial can overwhelm the need to challenge management.

Be comfortable with being outvoted. Strong people can get into a huff when their views don't carry the day. The right approach is to give total support to what is decided. Board work is the ultimate team sport. The coach says to Kobe Bryant, "I appreciate your insight, but you're not going to get the ball every time. Now be a team player."

Parfet: Board service is teamwork. No pigeonholing into roles or specialties or representing just one dimension. All directors should be ready to serve on all issues, contribute on all matters. It is important to create time during board meetings when the directors can be just among themselves to ensure shared understandings, determine if there are gaps in expectations and determine whether any issues need to be further examined. It is important to create an environment of openness in which people will participate and express themselves.

Murphy: There are board failings to be avoided, including conflicts of interest. The big disasters all had them. Complacency is a problem, getting too comfortable with management, strategy, failing to push the envelope. Lack of diversity in thought and opinion and insufficient focus on risk can be issues.

Jackson: Transparency by management is essential. The board has to know what is going on all the time, the good and the bad. Some boards don't allow for open discussion. Everything should be open for the board to discuss.

Hill: I want the board to be candid with me. It's easy for CEOs to believe their press. You need the board to be candid, raise questions, ask if you're sure, etc. I differentiate this from a director who Monday morning quarterbacks. I don't want that. Challenge is vital.

Halperin: Do an honest appraisal of the strengths and weaknesses of the company. Help management by identifying threats to and opportunities for the company. What current businesses can be disrupted by external factors? What can the company do to disrupt others? The Internet and globalization have been big disruptive factors, and there are and will be others.

The board should mentor and maintain open communication with management. Call and see them outside the office when their guard isn't up. A constant tension is that management needs to report things honestly but may feel that doing so will hurt the board's perception of their performance with consequences for their compensation, careers, etc. So it's important for the board to encourage honest reporting and transparency.

Downey: The board needs to be willing to talk about difficult things. Problem person. Performance issues. Succession. Stepping down. Dominance. Erratic behavior. Sometimes you have to go from the gut, not just the brain.

Bynoe: There are failings of boards and directors to be avoided. I think about smart people on boards who end up in bad situations, and I wonder, "What were they thinking? Were they afraid to speak up? Were they overly concerned about losing their seat at the table? Was there such an emphasis on teamwork that they did not want to dissent?" I have seen these things on boards, and they are a big red flag.

Directors must get a better understanding of risk and how it is linked to corporate strategy. It comes back to proper oversight of the

CEO and senior management and really understanding the business. People need to be empowered to speak up.

Boards need to be forward looking, have a long-term vision, and the board needs to put the right person in the CEO role with a succession plan.

What constitutes great governance?

Jackson: Ethical conduct must be top priority for every board.

Halperin: Leading management to discover, recognize, and cope with changes resulting from major threats and identifying opportunities. Take the financial crisis. No one could have predicted exactly what happened. We hadn't had a financial crisis in seventy-five years. It led to panic and a run on financial organizations and recession.

Great governance helped management think through this unprecedented situation. The best managers recognized that they were over-expanded and what they had to do to right-size asset levels, people, etc. Who are the right people with whom to go forward? Great companies deal with pain quickly then move ahead. Great governance was able to see this clearly and help guide through it and make hard decisions. Anticipate, understand, and adapt.

Bynoe: There are a lot of things boards must and should consider. But one size does not fit all. Board and management have to figure out the best structure and approach to enhance shareholder value and serve all stakeholders. For example, combining or separating the chair and CEO is situational. The same is true for compensation. What will encourage and incent people to give their best in achieving desired behaviors and outcomes? And for the committee structure—some committees are mandatory; others should be a function of company requirements and how best to balance the board's workload.

A key to great governance is collaboration and mutual respect among directors and with the senior leadership team. Without it, there will be dysfunction. You need to have the social issues in place— that leads to the right structure and processes and no factions.

The board needs to be probing and challenging. But at the end of the day, it needs to be supportive. Clear communication is required about what the board expects of senior management and vice versa. For example, what must be elevated to the board?

The board must define its risk appetite. Management recommends but the board has to support and be in alignment. If not, the board must insist on change.

Downey: Hire and retain the best possible CEO. Part of "best" is developing someone to follow in his or her footsteps. It's like successful coaches in sports—get and keep the person, create a culture. You can't do it with turnover every two or three years. Be realistic about CEO compensation. Someone making $50 or $60 million a year is egregious. So little is solely because of the individual—as a leader you're part of a team.

With a powerful CEO or chairman, be willing to stand up to him or her. The board is a system of contention, like a legal system. It's not perfect, but you have to believe it produces the best outcome most of the time. People who have all the answers scare the hell out of me.

Mullin: Understand whom you are protecting. In private companies, majority stockholders are on the board. So they are the voice in the room. They are driving things, so they don't need protection. What you want to do is challenge the majority stockholder's thinking in a graceful, thoughtful, supportive way. In public companies, shareholders are not in the room. So you need to represent them and protect their interests.

Hill: In today's environment, really stay focused on the company as opposed to all the external factors that are foisted on governance. Directors are so fearful of litigation that they can make decisions to ensure everything *looks* right versus *is* right. This can be an adverse effect of proxy advisory services. Directors need to make decisions based on the company's situation and needs, not what the proxy advisory services are looking for and saying.

There is not a cookie cutter for every corporation. Take Apple—I don't think anyone realizes how significant one individual was to an enterprise of that size. This is true of many technology companies. One or a handful of people makes the critical difference. Slavish adherence to pay guidelines risks disrupting these people. For example, the board may be criticized for the difference in pay between player A and player B, but it may be right and essential for that company.

Hall: Work for the shareholders, be prepared, help the CEO sort out tough challenges. Learn new skills. A board I'm on is immersing itself in information technology with IDEO, Stanford, etc. because the company is really an IT business in disguise.

Solso: When I took over as CEO at Cummins, we developed our guiding principles, including our vision, mission, values, and strategic principles. Our goal was to drive these elements down to the individual work plans of each employee. It was crucial that everyone in the company knew where we were going and how we were going to get there.

The directors were actively engaged in the development of our strategy and in supporting the vision, mission, and values. This was critical because the company was having serious financial challenges. For my first two years as CEO, Cummins was *in extremis*. I thought great governance was that our board stuck with management. Many boards would not have done so given the challenges we were facing. They had the patience and fortitude to stick with the leadership team because they understood what we were trying to do and believed in it.

So great governance is selecting the right CEO then having the patience, fortitude, and persistence to support that person through difficult times. Boards need to be very thoughtful about changing out management.

Great governance is also board willingness to do a deep dive into issues that require it, understanding there is no one right answer, and asking a lot of good questions. This is especially true for a company like Cummins, which has extensive business interests outside the United States.

For example, one Friday afternoon we got a call asserting that Cummins was selling engines into military equipment in Darfur, which was a human rights issue. We learned that our Chinese partner had done this. It was a very complex situation because while you don't have full control over a partner, you want to ensure your partner is acting in line with your values. The board worked its way through this delicate issue and ultimately supported management's handling of the affair.

While most of the issues the board is required to deal with are routine, some require more focus, time, and thoughtfulness than others. Great governance is recognizing the critical nature of certain issues and having a process to go after the facts and help management deal with situations in a very responsible way.

Siebel: The board serves two purses. First, they establish a punctuation point, a time by which management has to have its act together. Meetings create an opportunity for management to think through what's going on and present it, get plans tied off, etc.

Second, the board plays its most important role at times of crisis. That's when the board really has to perform. Crises happen all the time: management malfeasance, regulatory excess, competitive or market problems. This is when the board needs to step up and think things through. Mediocre boards throw the CEO under the bus, lawyer up, worry about themselves.

For example, the New York Stock Exchange board was a lowlight of corporate governance. When [CEO Richard] Grasso's compensation became controversial, they ran for the weeds. They were like a bunch of cockroaches. "We didn't know what the compensation plan was," etc. One director—Frank Langone—stood up. He was heroic, took Elliot Spitzer head on. That required courage.

What are the qualities that make for an excellent director?

Downey: First and foremost, you have to care. If you don't, you shouldn't do it—not for the money, not for the prestige, not for anything. If you are going to spend your time on something, it should be important to you.

Hill: Excellent directors have the requisite knowledge, skills, and ability, not just in the business but also in an array of areas important to the board. Also, they have an inquisitive nature about how things work. If you start with curiosity, you will want to learn about the company and make the effort to really understand the business, industry, and challenges faced.

Excellent directors are able to check their egos at the door. Nothing is more disruptive than a director who pontificates on a topic to convince everyone he or she is smart. Directors have been successful in life. Current and ex-CEOs tend to have strong egos, are used to being in charge. As directors, they are advisors and members of a team. They have the final say in little except replacing the CEO. If you can laugh at yourself and recognize your need to be in charge and that you're not, it can help you be an effective director.

One guy stands out in my mind. I joined the Arrow Electronics board eight years ago. The chairman was Dan Duval. His presence was all I needed to agree to join. I always felt that if I could find a model I wanted to move toward, it was Dan. He was incredibly smart and yet incredibly quiet. This is a very powerful combination. Dan was extremely good at sensing a situation, coalescing people's thoughts, and then making profound statements. He was always calm. He would always speak his mind. He was always in full command of what was going on and was able to add value in every situation—human, financial, technical. Maybe because he was different than I am—"often wrong but never in doubt!"—I found his approach inspiring.

Halperin: Excellent directors gain the respect of management and the other directors. They are direct and honest and able to communicate with respect and dignity the realities of the situation. They are insightful and able to break down complex issues into clear, understandable messages. Some of the best directors don't say a lot. But when they start to talk, everyone shuts up and listens.

Jim Harper [former EQR trustee] was excellent. Jim had a balance between quantitative and qualitative analysis, but he led with a qualitative analysis that gave context to the matters being discussed.

Hall: One director asks great questions. Another tends to have a different take on things and makes great suggestions. I know a CEO who stayed on the board after stepping down. He helped a lot in dealing with an unfriendly shareholder proposal. Asked good, hard questions.

Bynoe: Let me be personal. I enjoy being an independent director. It is an important role. I enjoy the intellectual stimulation and collegial work.

Curiosity is important—a desire to understand the business, company, and management. There is a lot of material to absorb—you have to prioritize. An excellent director can synthesize a lot of data and decide what is important, then figure out how to use what he or she has learned by being creative and thoughtful in the boardroom. Not grandstanding; rather, initiating to enhance and advance the dialogue.

Part of it is being a team player, but you also have to have the confidence and desire to be independent so you are not part of groupthink. You have to be willing to speak your mind, back it up, and disagree without being disagreeable. Find a way to be a consensus builder. It is important that when you have something to say, people listen—a result of the credibility you have built.

Solso: My best directors were advisors who asked tough questions that made me think about issues in ways that I might not have initially considered. They helped me do my job better. They were also mentors in my early years.

Good directors are totally engaged in and committed to the success of the company and its people. Good directors know when and where to engage and know the difference in helping the board make policy as opposed to running operations. Good directors are much more than watchdogs. If directors don't trust management to do the right thing, then they have a much bigger issue. Cummins was very fortunate to have several outstanding directors.

Siebel: An excellent director is active in his or her engagement model. Attends board meetings. Shows up on time. Is well prepared. Is active in finding ways to assist the company outside formal board meetings. Is thoughtful and creative at times of business crisis. Excellent directors take the role seriously and will not accept a position as a director unless willing to commit the time and energy necessary to assist the organization.

Eric Schmidt was a great director at Siebel Systems. Consistently prepared. Understood the business. Very thoughtful. Always asked penetrating questions, frequently questions that seemed about seven degrees out at the time, with the effect of making management think outside the box. Mike McCaffrey is an excellent director at C3 Energy. Provides both formal and informal board leadership. Expects excellence from the management team. He participates actively in helping think through tough problems.

Murphy: Engaged and participative but not domineering. Has the courage to speak one's mind. Leveraging special knowledge and openness to the knowledge of others. Stays current in own growth and development.

One other thing: the best directors are people who really understand the business and where it is going and are able to help accelerate movement toward the future. They bring prior knowledge and experience and apply it in the context of the company's business.

Mullin: Excellent directors are always prepared. They engage in far-ranging thinking. They're curious. They protect the stockholder first. They speak up. They support board decisions.

Jackson: Knowing when to leave. I left boards because I felt after some years that someone else needed to sit in the chair. Loved the experience, time to move on.

What are shortcomings and weaknesses you've seen in directors?

Bynoe: It is so apparent when directors come to meetings and are not fully prepared. They ask questions that are covered in the material. Everyone is busy; it is egalitarian. You need to come prepared. There is no compensatory model—I did not need to read that portion of the materials because I knew you would. A weakness is when everyone is not pulling his or her weight. Spend the requisite time at task.

Not understanding the culture. Every company has a culture, a way of interacting, collaborating, respecting, being part of the team. Directors need to understand the social dynamic or they will be less effective than they could be.

Directors who say they will serve on the board but do not have time to chair a committee. Being asked to chair a committee is an honor and an important role that elevates your leadership skills and provides better access to a more robust flow of information. If you are on the board, you should be prepared to do it.

Some directors utilize their board seats to enhance their business portfolio. I do not have a problem with this except when they are so concerned about maintaining their seats that they are unwilling to challenge or dissent. It compromises their independence.

Siebel: Inattentive. Not prepared. Willing to be misled by management. Don't make the effort to understand the business.

The most serious failing of boards relates to the failure to provide governance and oversight. Choosing to look the other way when it is obvious that a management change is necessary. Allowing the management team to execute critical policy decisions absent substantive board discussion and review. Allowing themselves to be manipulated by management.

Parfet: Directors who come to serve themselves. Accept the pay and prestige but don't want to dig in and face hard decisions. Don't work to develop the management team. Self-centered versus serving.

Murphy: Disengaged, unprepared, don't take the time to reflect on material in terms of what it means. Too concerned with what management and board colleagues think of them. Dominating the conversation. Too long with one company, one board, so it becomes rote or the frustration level is high—worn out.

Mullin: Lazy thinking; too supportive of management; haven't done enough homework to really understand the company.

Hill: Monday morning quarterbacking, not checking egos at the door, acting like they are in charge when they're not.

I think it's a mistake for boards to select directors to fill some social need instead of what the business needs. Diverse boards are great, but achieving it is difficult, especially in technology. It's a big mistake to get tired of looking and settle. You should never settle to achieve cosmetic diversity versus real intellectual diversity. If you find yourself making that choice, you will create disruption on the board. I'm pro-diversity, anti-settling.

Halperin: Directors who dominate the conversation without adding to the debate. Directors who try to demonstrate how important they are. Directors who try to gain advantage for themselves or friends through related party transactions and situations, though this is more under control now than it used to be. Seeking high director compensation by overcompensating the CEO and management to create a reciprocal dynamic.

Hall: Someone who takes a check-the-boxes approach. "It's best practice, therefore we should do it." Also, a predictable point of view based on functional expertise or emotional predisposition. For example, some directors are always positive or always negative. They don't think things through. Rest of board tunes out. They don't add anything.

Downey: (1) They want the job too badly. The pay and perquisites are good, so they try to support or stay out of the way of senior management who are influential in who stays on versus leaves the board. (2) Violating confidentiality. Talking about business outside the appropriate place. When you see this, you become cautious about sharing information. (3) Not doing their homework, not prepared when they go to a meeting. (4) Not willing to listen. Everyone wants to talk. (5) Demeanor. Some people like to intimidate, keep others from sharing. You never know where a good thought is going to come from. Everyone loses. (6) Lack of common courtesy and respect. (7) Not knowing when and how to quit. Staying too long. Needing to have the last word, a parting shot, throw it over their shoulder on the way out the door.

What are danger signals that you watch for on a board?

Solso: As a board member, I want full transparency from management. Not laying all the facts on the table or acting with an inadequate sense of urgency when warranted (e.g., violations of the Foreign Corrupt Practices Act) are all danger signs. I always assume when I see accounting problems that where there is smoke, there is fire.

Siebel: If management is consistently not prepared, if management is providing planning and direction that is not cohesive, if management appears to be less than candid in briefing the board and the board is not requiring answers to penetrating questions and requiring further disclosure, then the board is failing to do its job.

Parfet: If I hear someone say, "Well, you didn't ask that question, that's why I didn't disclose the information," this is very serious. Withholding information is a real violation of team play.

Murphy: When small groups of directors make major decisions and enter the room with decisions made. Lack of candor and failure to challenge or question management or one another. Conflicts of interest. Company performance lagging peers without sufficient inquiry or response—how we are doing relative to market, competitors, and why? Failure to evaluate performance of the board and individual directors.

Bynoe: The years since the financial crisis have been an important period to see how boards and CEOs communicate. What did management choose to escalate to the board? The information flow has to be right. There needs to be a high comfort level that the CEO and board are not out of touch in terms of what they expect from each other. I have never seen a situation where too much information created lasting problems, but I have seen the opposite. Inadequate information can permanently impair trust.

An imperial CEO is a red flag for me—a CEO who sees having a board as another obligation with which he or she has to contend. The CEO must appreciate the purpose and role of the board and act accordingly.

Mullin: It's not just the board. There are danger signals with management, like no succession plan in place or a process to get there. When you ask a question, you get a doubletalk answer.

Jackson: Management hiding employees from the board. It's a control issue. Conflicts between what you hear at the cocktail party versus what is said in the board meeting. Contradictions between leadership and authority. For example, if the COO has a larger voice in financial matters than the CFO, that suggests a problem.

When the minutes don't reflect the discussion. I make a point of reading minutes carefully and thinking about what the intention was and what was reported. There should be an accurate record of what was discussed. It creates a bridge to revisit certain issues after everyone has a chance to cool off and rethink it.

Halperin: Financial discrepancies and poor records. Management covering up shortfalls or making excuses. Management trying to keep opinions of their direct reports from reaching the board. Ethical violations—Foreign Corrupt Practices Act, sexual harassment.

When something doesn't look right or is askew, look into it. Sometimes boards just don't want to deal with things—for example, Penn State. Where there's smoke, there's fire.

Hall: Groupthink. By groupthink I mean the group tends to take the average of all the opinions, standardizes on it, doesn't look at outliers and contingencies. No one will catch all the black swans, but if you don't look for them you won't find them.

It's vital to pull out diverse views. My practice as lead director is to go around in executive session and require everyone to speak and add to the discussion.

Downey: Leaving the most important discussions to last. You should deal with the most important things first, when you're fresh and have the time.

What advice do you have for new directors?

Halperin: Slowly enter the conversation. Learn about the company: history, business, management, industry, and competitors. New directors need to gain insights into the other directors, their personalities, skill sets, etc. Do you trust them? Learn about the people you're with.

Remember that the board is a deliberative body, and there aren't many, for example, appeals courts, the U.S. Senate, juries. The purpose of a deliberative body is for a group to think about the same thing at the same time, try to reach consensus about the facts being considered, and then reach a judgment.

Hall: Go through a thoughtful company and governance orientation. Go to a seminar for board members including a financial analysis session. Keep your mouth shut for a while.

Downey: Be the person you are. Look inside yourself and be consistently who you are. Don't try to be somebody else. Don't try to be impressive.

Pay attention and listen. Don't think you are going to change the organization the day you show up. Earn the respect of board colleagues. Do this by doing the job you were hired to do, especially the difficult aspects.

Speak to the obvious. If you don't understand, take the risk and say so. People pretend like crazy and nod their heads, but sometimes they don't understand and are not willing to say so.

Solso: Pick the right board—it's hard to get off boards once you have joined. Ask yourself, "Is this a company and business that is interesting where I will be able to learn and make contributions? What are the company's values?" Look at other board members; what are they like? Ask about the big issues. Do plenty of due diligence. Spend quality time with senior management people. Do a lot of listening and little talking in your early meetings. Usually there is a pecking order and corporate culture. Don't come in trying to prove yourself.

Siebel: Take the time to develop a good understanding of the essentials of the business. What does it do? How does it work? What is the big picture? What constitutes success in the long run?

Parfet: Get to know the other directors—their life experiences, what makes them tick. Understand the business. How is value generated in the enterprise, and what strategic levers does management have available? Get into the routines of board work—plans, budgets, compensation, etc. Figure out where you need any extra help, and then go meet with appropriate management.

Murphy: Learn the business and strategy. Learn the board culture. Invest time in getting to know the senior management group and fellow directors. Find your voice sooner rather than later. Fresh perspective is valuable.

Jackson: New directors should listen and learn. Be attentive. We had a celebrity board member. She was wonderful, but she would step out for fifteen- to thirty-minute phone calls and would be working on scripts during the meeting. I wondered, "Why does she even bother to come?" If you bring another company's problems to the board meeting, you're stealing this company's money.

Directors need to see operations and visit customers. Learn the company. Read all the material including past minutes carefully. Remember that there are no dumb questions. If you're a smart person and you don't understand, you're not the only one. You may just be the only one speaking up.

Hill: Check your ego at the door. Make sure you trust the CEO and that he or she is honest. Work as hard in your responsibilities as a director as you do in your own job.

What do you think of the governance reforms of recent years?

Jackson: When I started, it was very clear: it was an old boys' network. I think everyone knew that it was an insiders' game. That has changed a lot for the better. Great governance in those days was totally based on trust, and by and large it worked, which is a tribute to the character of most of the people involved.

There was a complete lack of diversity. Everybody looked like the guy sitting at the head of the table. Mostly white, male, Christian. That has changed a lot over twenty years. In those days the great meals, airplanes, etc. were payback for support of the chairman/CEO. A director was almost never removed unless he disagreed with the chairman.

Another change is the role of the management. When I started, you almost never saw them except at parties. The chairman wanted to control information flow. A few handpicked executives came in to brief the board, and they were drilled pretty carefully about what to say and not to say to directors. Now we see much more of the management, which has created more transparency.

The chairman/CEO was not always viewed as the best to lead the company in terms of shareholder value but rather the best to keep the company out of trouble. That has changed.

With regard to legislation, Sarbanes-Oxley had to happen. Some companies were on a self-destruction path. Anyone who thought all the problems would work themselves out was naïve. The cost and burdens have been tremendous but the value to shareholders and our economic system has been worthwhile. There was a lot of complaining, but the legislation was worthwhile. It's like putting speed signs up on a highway: sometimes you have to save people from themselves.

The returns are still out on Dodd-Frank. It came about because some companies were not being honest, were not sharing information, were abusing shareholders and taxpayers. I'm not sure Dodd-Frank is the answer, but we'll see.

One other thing: I believe in terms limits for boards. I think you start to lose something after five or six years, maybe longer. Need to get fresh ideas and thinking on the board. There has to be a way of getting people off the board.

Solso: Most CEOs don't like the reforms. My view is that they are a reality and a predictable reaction to problems like excessive compensation, accounting fraud, and corporate implosions. Regulators are stakeholders. Get in and work with them like Cummins did with the Environmental Protection Agency. Try to make regulations as responsible as you can, not just watered-down laws that suit your individual needs. Don't automatically reject what they are trying to do just because regulations can be costly and complex. I am convinced we have cleaner air and water as a result of the Environmental Protection Agency, and that benefits everyone in the long run.

Sarbanes-Oxley was an overreaction, but I can say that at Cummins accounting is much better because of SOX. However, instead of creating more accessible and transparent information, Sarbanes-Oxley has created a more legalistic and expensive environment. That works to nobody's benefit.

Siebel: Dodd-Frank was an inflection point in corporate governance. Before Dodd-Frank, board meetings were focused on markets, customers, shareholders, and strategic planning. Post Dodd-Frank, the preponderance of board and management attention in many public companies has become absorbed with assuring that the company has properly complied with nonproductive regulatory requirements involving burdensome documentation of all the ways the company has mitigated business risk. With the advent of Dodd-Frank, business and market risk became something to avoid and mitigate at all cost rather than a business opportunity to tackle and leverage to create market value.

Also, the objective of financial reporting is clarity and transparency. The effect of many disclosure and reporting requirements has been to complicate and obfuscate financial condition. I challenge an SEC regulator or a member of Congress to read the financial reports of a J.P. Morgan Chase and explain what is happening. It is virtually impossible today to get a sense of the financial condition and prospects of a large public corporation by reading their financial statements, largely due to their need to comply with mandated reporting requirements. A simple and clear statement of the financial condition of a public corporation is inconsistent with regulatory and legislative mandates. We need to fix that.

The gap between the benefits of being a private company and the burdens of being public has never been greater.

Parfet: Better governance is a huge issue right now. Whether we needed legislative action following the Enron collapse or just to be told the Enron story is a good question. The main impact on directors is the story—a cautionary tale. Hearing the Enron story and learning from other failed companies are remarkable lessons in governance. Watch the movie. Same with *Barbarians at the Gate*. That goes much further than legislation and regulation.

Murphy: Corporate governance has improved. While I can point to specific things that are not cost effective, in general, there is a higher level of awareness and interest in governance and practices have improved because of these forces for change.

For example, the SEC executed Section 404 [of Sarbanes-Oxley] poorly. There was a lot of consternation among auditors and CFOs. But 404 has been very positive in raising the awareness level of the control environment in companies. Section 404 was poorly executed and expensive but valuable.

The pendulum has been swinging toward more control, probably too much. There's uncertainty about Dodd-Frank. There should be more care with new legislation and regulation—less sweeping and more targeted. Nonetheless, governance has improved. Some is due to activist investors. It's costly and distracting but increases awareness of good governance practices. I'm always looking to make lemonade out of lemons: find the good and manage the negative.

Hill: I was chairman during this period of reform. The benefit is that it institutionalized and broadened some good practices like executive sessions. We did them, but not everyone did. And it has made these practices routine and habitual. So when you get into urgent, pressurized situations, this is the way you operate.

But when it comes to reform, be careful what you wish for. The biggest mistake being made now is that people want to take risk out of investing. If a loss occurs, that's failure. Case in point: J.P. Morgan, Jamie Dimon, the London Whale. Business involves taking risks, which entails losses at times. The notion that "that should never happen" is a problem. If the Whale had hit a homerun, we never would have heard about it. The Whale problem did not endanger J.P. Morgan. Dimon is an outstanding chairman and CEO. For anyone to tie the Whale incident to separating the roles makes no sense. Investing by its nature has risk associated with it. Return is related to risk. There's no risk without occasional loss. The Whale trade was internal to the operation. You have to look at the totality of results.

The market is very efficient, so when writing legislation, you have to ask what are you trying to achieve that will really improve things.

Hall: I am a big fan of Sarbanes-Oxley. Even though people complained about the costs, it helped even good companies develop far better internal controls. The challenge now is to keep it a vibrant process rather than a checklist.

I wonder about binding say-on-pay like in the United Kingdom. It might be a good idea. It may be the only hope we have of getting control of executive compensation. We have made progress in pay for performance, but I think we pay senior people too much relative to what we need to pay.

I'm a big fan of having a lead director or strong nonexecutive chairman (and not the former CEO). Executive sessions without management are a big improvement. I like to have them at the beginning and end of meetings.

I favor board succession planning, term limits—about twelve years seems right—and no mandatory retirement age. I understand the tradeoffs. I favor term limits to get people off the board in order to get new people in. Keep it fresh. The problem with a mandatory retirement age is waivers. People are staying healthy and vibrant; they don't want to leave, and others don't want them to.

Bynoe: Reforms are a cost of doing business in the public arena. Once trust is broken, change is inevitable, and it takes time to rebuild. Have the reforms been worthwhile? It is hard to know with certainty. Our job as directors is to make governance better. We need to be compliant. We ask for public investment and support, so let's find a way to make reforms useful in running our businesses better and reassuring investors that their companies are in good hands.

At the end of the day, regulations can be put in place, but it all comes back to quality people in a culture that encourages pushback, challenge, using common sense. If it does not seem right, question it. Every director has a role to play and needs to have the courage to stand up and be heard. This is best way to reduce failure and fraud and keep problems as sidelines rather than headlines.

CHAPTER 8

Conclusion

The "Vital Few" for Boards and Directors

When Kaoru Ishikawa, Japan's great quality expert, visited Cummins to share his thinking with senior management, he introduced me to a term I've never forgotten: the *vital few* versus the *trivial many*. Quality, Dr. Ishikawa told us, always depends on focus on the former and not being distracted by the latter. This is as true for boards as any other work group.

In the preceding chapters, I have shared my thinking on how corporate and nonprofit boards and directors can be good stewards and achieve great governance. To summarize my *vital few* messages:

- Be great cathedral builders in addition to competent bricklayers.

- Maintain the organization's ability to control its destiny (i.e., its right of self-determination).

- Maximize long-term economic value creation (companies) and efficient mission achievement (nonprofits).

- Insist on a foundation of broad excellence and pursue high aspirations and vision.

- Understand the role of directors and the board. Practice stewardship thinking. Govern rather than manage. Help as well as monitor.

- Develop a deep understanding of the enterprise. It means many things to many people. It is a story with chapters completed and more to be written.

- Do the right things. Ensure the substance of board work is on the mark. Appoint a great leader, ensure a smart strategy and effective execution, maintain a prudent risk profile, and set a tone of integrity at the top.

- Do things right. Ensure directors have quality information. Create a process that enables the board to deliberate and debate consequential matters and make rational decisions. Get out of the *boardroom bubble*.

- Embrace what is best in good governance: board independence, transparency, accountability, and renewal; frequent executive sessions; equity ownership and pay-for-performance. Be skeptical of unsupported assertions, one-size-fits-all orthodoxy, and a checklist approach.

In the previous chapter, I reported on the governance views of experienced directors. These people are not shrinking violets, and they don't agree on everything. Some, for example, see net benefit in governance reforms while others see high cost and problematic consequences. Still, there is broad consensus on some important matters:

- Governance has improved because of greater focus on shareholder value, use of equity incentives, transparency, independence of directors from management, and prevalence of executive sessions.

- The board's monitoring function is a given. Deep value lies in the board's assisting management to build a vibrant, successful enterprise. Some issues deserve a deep dive by the board. The board has a vital role in successfully navigating crises.

- A board's most important duties are in strategy, leadership, and risk.

- Basics matter in director effectiveness: preparation, attendance, engagement, and contribution. No smartphones in laps!

- Challenge and debate are essential to good strategy and decisions. Politics and factions are destructive to good board process. Big ego and high maintenance directors are unwelcome.

- A board is a portfolio of talents, experiences, and career stages. The common focus is shared stewardship of the company or organization.

- New directors should learn the business, get to know the senior people, listen a lot, be themselves, and learn how to help the board get things done.

- Smaller boards, lead directors, and executive sessions help increase candor and debate among directors.

- Corporate directors represent owners. Their primary focus must be long-term economic value creation.

- There are many more similarities than differences in the stewardship of various kinds of organizations: public and private companies and nonprofits. But the differences that do exist—in stakeholders, ownership, authority, performance metrics—are important for governance.

- Success and complacency plant seeds of decline. The board is obliged to raise sights and challenge the status quo to lay the groundwork for continued success.

- Failing to initiate or adapt to disruptive change can lead to decline and failure. Directors need to help management get ahead of the curve.

- Respect is the coin of the realm in the boardroom. Directors earn it through a sustained record of thoughtful consideration, competence, and contribution.

- A board seat is not a sinecure. Turnover is necessary for board renewal. Board succession should be like a well-run relay race: carefully planned with some overlap, a minimum of lost speed, and no dropped batons.

I began this book by introducing you to two great companies with which I have had the longest governance experience: Gordon Food Service and Equity Residential.

In both cases, I have had the deeply satisfying experience of working with board colleagues to provide governance that has enabled the companies to thrive, create a lot of economic value, and maintain control of their destinies. A remaining task for those of us who have been in governance of these companies for a long time is to ensure smooth and orderly succession—passing the baton without missing a beat. That work is well underway.

Governance is interesting, challenging, rewarding, and fun. I hope my messages will help boards and directors become more effective in their work and, as a result, better stewards of the enterprises with which they are entrusted. Those organizations, as well as America and the world, will be better for it.

Notes

[1] Many real estate investment trusts (REITs), such as EQR, are formed as trusts under Maryland law, so their boards are composed of trustees instead of directors even though their functions are identical.

[2] Platt, Suzy, ed., *Respectfully Quoted: A Dictionary of Quotations* (New York: Barnes & Noble Books, 1993).

[3] Kopp, Wendy, Official Biography, Teach for America website, October 15, 2012. http://www.teachforamerica.org.

[4] Isaacson, Walter, *Steve Jobs* (New York: Simon & Schuster, 2011).

[5] Greenleaf, Robert; Spears, Larry; and Stephen Covey, *Servant Leadership: A Journey into the Nature of Legitimate Power and Greatness*, 25th Anniversary Edition (Mahway, NJ: Paulist Press, 2002).

[6] *The Bible*, New Testament, Mark 10:45 (New International Version).

[7] Depree, Max, *Leadership is an Art* (East Lansing, MI: Michigan State University Press, 1987).

[8] "Director Liability in the Wake of the WorldCom and Enron Settlements." *Howard Rice Alert*, February 25, 2005.

[9] Stout, Lynn, *The Shareholder Value Myth* (San Francisco: Berrett-Koehler Publishers, 2012) provides spirited and thoughtful arguments against the primacy of shareholder interests for boards.

[10] Gillespie, John, and David Zweig, *Money for Nothing* (New York: Free Press, 2010).

[11] "4 Things You Don't Know About Private Companies." *Forbes*, May 26, 2013.

[12] Mader, Steve, and Kerry Moynihan, "Governance at Controlled Public Companies." *Corporate Board*, November 1, 2005.

[13] *Controlled Companies in the Standard and Poor's 1500: A Ten-Year Performance and Risk Review.* IRRC Institute and ISS, October 2012, http://irrcinstitute.org/pdf/FINAL-Controlled-Company-ISS-Report.pdf.

[14] *The Management of Berkshire Hathaway*, Case CG-16, Rock Center for Corporate Governance, Stanford Graduate School of Business, January 1, 2009, 19.

[15] Ibid.

[16] Kerr, Clark, *The Uses of the University: Fifth Edition* (Cambridge, MA: Harvard University Press, 2002).

[17] Spar, Debra, and Jennifer Burns, *Hitting the Wall: Nike and International Labor Practices* (Cambridge, MA: Harvard Business School Publications, Product #7000-47-PDF-ENG, January 19, 2000).

[18] Katz, D., and R. L. Kahn, *The Social Psychology of Organizations* (New York: John Wiley & Sons, 1966).

[19] Mautz, Robert K., *Internal Control in U.S. Corporations: The State of the Art* (New York: Financial Executives Research Foundation, 1980).

[20] White, B. Joseph, *The Nature of Leadership: Reptiles, Mammals and the Challenge of Becoming a Great Leader* (New York: AMACOM, 2007).

[21] Hoffman, Bruce G., *American Icon: Alan Mulallay and the Fight to Save Ford Motor Company* (New York: Crown Publishing Group, 2012).

[22] Porter, Michael, *Competitive Strategy* (New York: Free Press, 1980).

[23] Prahalad, C.K., *The Fortune at the Bottom of the Pyramid: Eradicating Poverty through Profits*, Revised Edition (Philadelphia: Wharton School Publishing, 2009).

[24] "Executive Pay by the Numbers," Business Day, *New York Times*, June 29, 2013, http://www.nytimes.com/interactive/2013/06/30/business/executive-compensation-tables.html?_r=0.

[25] Frank, Robert H., and Philip J. Cook, *The Winner-Take-All Society: Why the Few at the Top Get So Much More Than the Rest of Us* (London: Penguin Books, 1996).

[26] Gabaix, Savier, and Augustin Landier, "Why Has CEO Pay Increased So Much?" *Quarterly Journal of Economics* 123:1 (2008): 49–100.

[27] Kaplan, Steven N., and Joshua Rauh, "Wall Street and Main Street: What Contributes to the Rise in the Highest Incomes?" *Review of Financial Studies* 23:3 (2010): 1004–50.

[28] Kindleberger, Charles P., *Manias, Panics, and Crashes: A History of Financial Crises* (Hoboken, NJ: John Wiley & Sons, 2005).

[29] "Cummins Inc. Stock Buy Recommendation Reiterated (CMI)." *TheStreet*, October 17, 2012. http://www.thestreet.com/story/11739717/1/cummins-inc-stock-buy-recommendation-reiterated-cmi.html.

[30] Collins, Jim, *How the Mighty Fall: And Why Some Companies Never Give In* (Jim Collins, 2009).

[31] Christensen, Clayton M., *The Innovator's Dilemma* (Boston: Harvard Business School Press, 1997).

[32] "David Alger is Dead at 57; Manager of Mutual Funds," Business Day, *New York Times*, September 25, 2001.

[33] Moeller, Sara; Schlingemann, Frederik; and Rene Stulz, *Do Shareholders of Acquiring Firms Gain from Acquistions?* NBER Working Paper No. 9523.

[34] Schein, Edgar H., *Humble Inquiry: The Gentle Art of Asking Instead of Telling* (San Francisco: Berrett-Koehler Publishers, 2013).

[35] "Why Teams Don't Work: An Interview with J. Richard Hackman," *Harvard Business Review*, May 2009.

[36] Larcker, David, and Brian Tayan, *Corporate Governance Matters* (Upper Saddle River, NJ: FT Press, 2011).

[37] Kahneman, Daniel, *Thinking Fast and Slow* (New York: Farrar, Straus and Giroux, 2010).

[38] Halberstam, David, *The Best and the Brightest* (New York: Ballantine Books, 20th Anniversary Edition, 2003).

[39] "Citigroup Chief Stays Bullish on Buyouts." *Financial Times*, July 9, 2007.

[40] Simon, Herbert, *Administrative Behavior*, 4th Edition (New York: Free Press, 1997).

[41] Gigerenzer, G., and R. Selten, eds., *Bounded Rationality: The Adaptive Toolbox* (Cambridge, MA: The MIT Press, 2001).

[42] Dietrich, J. Richard; Kachelmeier, Steven J.; Kleinmuntz, Don N.; and Thomas J. Linsmeier, "Market Efficiency, Bounded Rationality and Supplemental Business Reporting Disclosures." *Journal of Accounting Research* 39:2 (September 2001): 243–68.

[43] An NBC poll taken in 2004 reported that although 77 percent of 1,186 people sampled thought Simpson was guilty, only 27 percent of blacks in the sample believed so, compared to 87% of whites.

[44] Hales, Jeffrey, "Directional Preferences, Information Processing, and Investors' Forecasts of Earnings." *Journal of Accounting Research* 45:3 (June 2007): 607–28.

[45] Libby, Robert, and Kristina Rennekamp, "Self-Serving Attribution Bias, Overconfidence, and the Issuance of Voluntary Disclosures." *Journal of Accounting Research* 50:1 (March 2012): 197–231.

[46] Lehrer, Jonah, "Groupthink." *The New Yorker*, January 2012, 22–27.

[47] Kahneman, Daniel; Lovallo, Dan; and Olivier Sibony, "Before You Make That Big Decision." *Harvard Business Review*, June 2011.

[48] Lovallo, Dan, and Olivier Sibony, "The Case for Behavioral Strategy." *McKinsey Quarterly* 2 (2010): 30–43.

[49] The U.S. Supreme Court in 2005 unanimously reversed the conviction, but it was too late to save the firm.

[50] Sonnenfeld, Jeffrey. "What Makes Great Boards Great?" *Harvard Business Review*, September 2002.

[51] Keinath, Annemarie K., and Judith C. Walo, "Audit Committee Responsibilities: Focusing on Oversight, Open Communication and Best Practices." *The CPA Journal Online*, November 2004. http://www.nysscpa.org/cpajournal/2004/1104/essentials/p22.htm.

[52] Following shareholder votes on "say when on pay" in 2011, many public companies now provide for an annual shareholder say-on-pay vote.

[53] "Court Deals Blow to SEC, Activists." *Wall Street Journal*, July 23, 2011. http://online.wsj.com/news/articles/SB1000142405311 1903554904576461932431478332.

[54] "What the New Proxy Access Rules Mean for You." *Corporate Secretary*, February 1, 2012.

[55] GMI Ratings website, http://www3.gmiratings.com/home/.

[56] GMI Ratings_ESGWhitepaper_062012.pdf, http://www3.gmi-ratings.com/home/white-papers/.

[57] Global Industry Classification 4040 is the financial industry, real estate sector.

[58] Gompers, Paul; Ishii, Joy; and Andrew Metrick, "Corporate Governance and Equity Prices." *Quarterly Journal of Economics* 118:1 (February 2003): 107–55.

[59] Larcker, David, and Brian Tayan, *Corporate Governance Matters* (Upper Saddle River, NJ: Pearson Prentice Hall, 2011), 15.

[60] Bebchuk, Lucian; Cohen, Alma; and Allen Ferrell, "What Matters in Corporate Governance?" *Review of Financial Studies* 22:2 (February 2009): 783–827.

[61] Larcker and Tayan, *Corporate Governance Matters*, 15.

[62] Ibid., 160.

[63] Ibid.

[64] Nadler, David, "The Argument for a Separate Chair" in Jay Lorsch, ed., *The Future of Boards: Meeting the Governance Challenges of the Twenty-First Century* (Boston: Harvard Business School Press, 2012).

[65] Hanafee, Susan, *Red, Black and Global: The Transformation of Cummins* 1995–2010.

[66] "Stocks Perform Better if Women Are on Company Boards." *Bloomberg News.* http://mobile.bloombeerg.com/news/2012-07-31/women-as-directors-beat-men-only-boards-in-company-stock-return.html.

[67] Lois, Joy; Carter, Nancy; Wagner, Harvey; and Sriram Narayanan, "The Bottom Line: Corporate Performance and Women's Representation on Boards," Catalyst, Inc., 2007.

[68] Burgstahler, David, and Ilia Dichev, "Earnings Management to Avoid Earnings Decreases and Losses." *Journal of Accounting and Economics* 24:1 (1997): 99–126.

[69] Larcker, David, and Brian Tayan, *Corporate Governance Matters*, 330.

[70] Armstrong, Chris S.; Ittner, Christopher D.; and David F. Larcker, "Corporate Governance, Compensation Consultants, and CEO Pay Levels." *Review of Accounting Studies* 17:2 (2012): 322–51.

[71] Core, John E.; Holthausen, Robert W.; and David F. Larcker, "Corporate Governance, Chief Executive Officer Compensation and Firm Performance." *Journal of Financial Economics* 51:3 (1999): 371–406.

[72] Larcker, David, and Brian Tayan, *Corporate Governance Matters*, 282.

[73] Ibid., 15.

[74] Ibid., 459–60.

[75] Steele, Myron, "Verbatim: 'Common Law Should Shape Governance.'" *NACD Directorship*, February 15, 2010.

Acknowledgments

Many people contributed to my ability to write this book.

I am grateful to the Gordon family and my colleagues on the GFS board. Thank you to my current colleagues on the EQR board, former colleagues Jim Harper, Sheli Rosenberg, and Ed Lowenthal, and General Counsel Bruce Strohm. I have learned much from fellow directors at Kelly Services, M Financial, the Upjohn Institute, and other corporate and nonprofit boards on which I have served.

I thank the directors I was privileged to interview: Chuck Atwood, Linda Walker Bynoe, Dave Downey, Dan Gordon, Jim Gordon, Dave Gray, Errol Halperin, Bill Hall, Rick Hill, Mannie Jackson, Peter Mullin, Leslie Murphy, David Neithercut, Don Parfet, Tom Siebel, Tim Solso, and Sam Zell.

I extend a heartfelt thank you to Mary Kay Haben, who agreed to review chapter drafts, and Jane Dutton, who introduced and endorsed me to Berrett-Koehler Publishers. Thank you to Keith Decie for helping disseminate the book's messages and to Kate Metz for helping me in many ways.

I appreciate the confidence and encouragement of colleagues at the University of Illinois, including President Bob Easter, Chancellor

Phyllis Wise, Provost Ade Adesida, Dean Larry Debrock, and Professors Joe Mahoney, Bill Qualls, Aric Rindfleisch, Madhu Viswanathan, Raj Echambadi, and Ruth Aguilera. I thank the business and law students in my U.S. Corporate Governance courses for their good work and interest in the subject.

My son, Brian, completed his PhD in accountancy, began his faculty career, and broadened my intellectual horizons as I wrote. My daughter, Audrey Imhoff, inspired me to work hard with her own hard work. My father and mother, Bernie and Gena White, died recently after seventy years of marriage and long, fulfilling lives. I am grateful for the values they instilled in me.

Most of all, I thank my wife, Mary, for her love and support.

Index

About the Author

B. Joseph (Joe) White is James F. Towey Professor of Business and Leadership and President Emeritus at the University of Illinois and Dean Emeritus of the Ross School of Business at the University of Michigan. He teaches U.S. corporate governance to graduate business and law students at Illinois. He is the author of *The Nature of Leadership: Reptiles, Mammals and the Challenge of Becoming a Great Leader* (AMACOM, 2007).

Joe is a trustee and chair of the corporate governance committee of Equity Residential, Inc. (NYSE:EQR). During his service, EQR has grown from an enterprise value of $800 million to over $30 billion, delivered annualized total shareholder return of 13 percent and become an S&P 500 company.

Joe is a director of Gordon Food Service. During his service, GFS has grown from $400 million to over $10 billion in revenue and become one of America's 40 largest private companies. He helped create governance arrangements intended to enable GFS to thrive in perpetuity as an independent family business.

Joe has extensive experience on corporate and nonprofit boards including Kelly Services, M Financial Holdings, W.E. Upjohn Institute for Employment Research, Argonne National Laboratory, American Council on Education, National Merit Scholarship Corporation and Georgetown University.

Joe was the sixteenth president of the University of Illinois from 2005–2009. He served as dean of the University of Michigan Business School (now the Ross School of Business) from 1991 to 2001. He has private sector experience, including six years as an officer of Cummins, Inc.

Joe brings to *Boards that Excel* background as an influential force in business education and talent development. As dean at Michigan, he integrated action learning into MBA studies, creating the first new curriculum model since introduction of the case method. Joe touched off movements in the business school world that elevated corporate citizenship and increased the ranks of women and minority executives.

In *Boards that Excel*, Joe blends governance research with practical experience and shows how to turn knowledge into action. He urges corporate and nonprofit directors to set high aspirations and provides practical advice on how to achieve them. He shares the wisdom of experienced directors through candid and insightful interviews.

Joe is a graduate of Georgetown University, Harvard Business School, and the University of Michigan. He and his wife, Mary, have two children and five grandchildren.

Berrett–Koehler
BK Publishers

Berrett-Koehler is an independent publisher dedicated to an ambitious mission: *Creating a World That Works for All*.

We believe that to truly create a better world, action is needed at all levels—individual, organizational, and societal. At the individual level, our publications help people align their lives with their values and with their aspirations for a better world. At the organizational level, our publications promote progressive leadership and management practices, socially responsible approaches to business, and humane and effective organizations. At the societal level, our publications advance social and economic justice, shared prosperity, sustainability, and new solutions to national and global issues.

A major theme of our publications is "Opening Up New Space." Berrett-Koehler titles challenge conventional thinking, introduce new ideas, and foster positive change. Their common quest is changing the underlying beliefs, mindsets, institutions, and structures that keep generating the same cycles of problems, no matter who our leaders are or what improvement programs we adopt.

We strive to practice what we preach—to operate our publishing company in line with the ideas in our books. At the core of our approach is stewardship, which we define as a deep sense of responsibility to administer the company for the benefit of all of our "stakeholder" groups: authors, customers, employees, investors, service providers, and the communities and environment around us.

We are grateful to the thousands of readers, authors, and other friends of the company who consider themselves to be part of the "BK Community." We hope that you, too, will join us in our mission.

A BK Business Book

This book is part of our BK Business series. BK Business titles pioneer new and progressive leadership and management practices in all types of public, private, and nonprofit organizations. They promote socially responsible approaches to business, innovative organizational change methods, and more humane and effective organizations.

Berrett–Koehler
Publishers

A community dedicated to creating
a world that works for all

Dear Reader,

Thank you for picking up this book and joining our worldwide community of Berrett-Koehler readers. We share ideas that bring positive change into people's lives, organizations, and society.

To welcome you, we'd like to offer you a free e-book. You can pick from among twelve of our bestselling books by entering the promotional code **BKP92E** here: http://www.bkconnection.com/welcome.

When you claim your free e-book, we'll also send you a copy of our e-newsletter, the *BK Communiqué*. Although you're free to unsubscribe, there are many benefits to sticking around. In every issue of our newsletter you'll find

- A free e-book
- Tips from famous authors
- Discounts on spotlight titles
- Hilarious insider publishing news
- A chance to win a prize for answering a riddle

Best of all, our readers tell us, "Your newsletter is the only one I actually read." So claim your gift today, and please stay in touch!

Sincerely,

Charlotte Ashlock
Steward of the BK Website

Questions? Comments? Contact me at bkcommunity@bkpub.com.

Certified

Corporation
bcorporation.net